—ODE TO GEN X—

ODE TO GEN X

INSTITUTIONAL CYNICISM IN STRANGER THINGS AND 1980S FILM

MELISSA VOSEN CALLENS

UNIVERSITY PRESS OF MISSISSIPPI / JACKSON

The University Press of Mississippi is the scholarly publishing agency of
the Mississippi Institutions of Higher Learning: Alcorn State University,
Delta State University, Jackson State University, Mississippi State University,
Mississippi University for Women, Mississippi Valley State University,
University of Mississippi, and University of Southern Mississippi.

www.upress.state.ms.us

The University Press of Mississippi is a member
of the Association of University Presses.

First printing 2021
∞

Library of Congress Control Number: 2021930385
Harback ISBN 978-1-4968-3241-2
Trade paperback ISBN 978-1-4968-3242-9
Epub single ISBN 978-1-4968-3243-6
Epub institutional ISBN 978-1-4968-3244-3
PDF single ISBN 978-1-4968-3245-0
PDF institutional ISBN 978-1-4968-3246-7

British Library Cataloging-in-Publication Data available

Contents

Acknowledgments vii

1   **You're the Inspiration**

Gen X and *Stranger Things*. 3

2   **What's Love Got to Do with It?**

Gen X and the Family Unit 23

3   **Opportunity (Let's Make Lots of Money)**

1980s American Economy. 59

4   **Fight the Power**

Gen X's Relationship with the Law and Government 97

5   **Can't Knock the Hustle**

Gen X as Adults. 123

6   **Conclusion** 159

Notes. 165

Works Cited 167

Index. 183

Acknowledgments

This book would not have been possible without the support I received from a variety of people. As such, I would like to thank them and the furry friends listed below.

Thank you to my husband, Nate Callens, who binged (and re-binged) with me *Stranger Things* and all of the films referenced in this book. Throughout this process, he listened thoughtfully to my observations and ongoing analysis, never complaining when I replayed a scene more than once. Additionally, he designed the book's cover. His cover perfectly captures the spirit of the book!

Thank you to the staff of the University Press of Mississippi. You all have been wonderful to work with, in particular Katie Keene. For her guidance during the process, I am grateful.

Thank you to my friend and colleague, Dr. Brian Hough, who started this project with me and served as a sounding board as I drafted each chapter.

Thank you to my colleagues at the Popular Culture Association who provided me with valuable feedback over the last couple of years. You have welcomed me to your area, generational studies, and I am thankful. I have learned so much from each and every one of you.

Thank you to my mom who, despite never seeing *Stranger Things*, asked about the project weekly, ultimately serving as my loudest cheerleader. When days were long and the project was stalled, she reminded me how much I have always enjoyed writing and how I have always enjoyed popular culture.

Thank you to my three devon rex cats: Huey Lewis, Joan Jett, and Stevie Nicks. They listened to many proofreads and provided me with snuggles when I needed them the most.

—ODE TO GEN X—

—1—
You're the Inspiration
Gen X and *Stranger Things*

It took some time to name the generation immediately succeed-
ing the Baby Boomer generation (1946–64), the generation
that would eventually be known as Generation X (Gen X). In
1993 generational scholars Neil Howe and Bill Strauss suggested
the name Thirteeners (in reference to the generation being the
thirteenth generation after the American Revolution), but the
name never quite stuck. In 1993 they published their first major
think piece about the unnamed cohort, calling it *13th Gen:
Abort, Retry, Ignore, Fail?* According to Howe and Strauss, the
subtitle was in reference to a computer's response to a missing
or damaged file. They chose this subtitle because they believed
it reflected how the country treated Gen Xers, seeing them as
"a missing or damaged generation" (Lavin). Even though Howe
and Strauss's proposed name was never widely used to describe
this generational cohort, *how* they described the generation
was. The descriptors "missing" and "forgotten" would come to
summarize not only the world's view of Gen X, but also Gen
X's view of themselves.

The lexical origins of Gen X are somewhat debatable. According to Raymond Gozzi, author of *The Power of Metaphor and New Words and a Changing American Culture*, "the first use of the phrase 'Generation X' was in the 1970s as the name of Billy Idol's band in London" (331). This, however, was not the first time the name was uttered. The name first appeared in a Robert Capa photo essay about coming-of-age teenagers after World War II (Raphelson), and Billy Idol attributed the name of his band (the more widely known reference) to a 1964 book titled *Generation X*. The book features candid interviews with postwar Baby Boomer teenagers and was authored by British journalists Jane Deverson and Charles Hamblet. Despite its popularity, the book was out of print by the late 1960s, and the phrase was all but extinct for nearly two decades.

Most credit the naming of the post–Baby Boom generation to Canadian author and artist Douglas Coupland, more specifically his 1991 novel *Generation X*. The inspiration for the book's title was not Idol's band as many at the time surmised; rather, the inspiration for his book was a 1983 academic book titled *Class: A Guide Through the American Status System* by literary historian Paul Fussell. Coupland reflects on that book: "In his final chapter, Fussell named an 'X' category of people who wanted to hop off the merry-go-round of status, money, and social climbing that so often frames modern existence. The citizens of X had much in common with my own socially disengaged characters; hence the title" ("Generation X'd"). Coupland believed the title reflected the spirit of his primary characters, as the "X" descriptor allowed his characters to be not only mysterious and complex individuals but also part of a larger disenfranchised group ("Generation X'd"). These qualities, he believed, accurately reflected young adults in the late 1980s and early 1990s.

In his novel, Coupland tells the stories of three Gen Xers as they struggle with their transition into adulthood. For example, in the novel the narrator describes an incident in which one of the main characters, Dag, vandalizes a car with graffiti: "The car was the color of butter and bore a bumper sticker saying WE'RE SPENDING OUR CHILDREN'S INHERITANCE, a message that I suppose irked Dag, who was bored and cranky after eight hours of working his McJob ('Low pay, low prestige, low benefits, low future')" (*Generation X*, 5). While the 1980s saw an increase in low-wage jobs, Gen Xers transitioning into adulthood, like Dag, were one of the groups that suffered most. Gen Xers often felt disadvantaged, particularly compared to their Boomer parents, as Gozzi states: "X'ers feel they were born too late. . . . All the good jobs are gone—taken by *Boomers*. . . . And they're supposedly less smart and talented than the older *Boomers*— declining SAT scores 'prove' that" (331). With parents who were either unable or unwilling to help financially, Gen Xers, blamed for their lack of "traditional" knowledge despite a shift in the country's educational system in which they had no control, were plagued by an absence of class mobility. Ultimately, these factors caused them to be *seen* as pessimistic about life.

Journalists have often described Gen X as cynical and materialistic (Hornblower), and other generations have used similar descriptions for Gen X. These descriptors were used not only in their youth. Some Millennials, for example, view middle-aged Gen Xers as "the most selfish and complaining generation, and the least heroic" (Howe and Strauss, *Millennials Rising*, 56). Despite this portrait, many Gen Xers object to these caricatures, arguing that they make "them feel labeled, stereotyped, unappreciated in their diversity" (Gozzi, 331). Liza Featherstone, in her 1994 write-up detailing entrepreneurialism among Gen X magazine start-ups, observed that while "marketers and the media are falling all over themselves trying to figure out who these new consumers are: Scotch drinkers? Kurt Cobain mourners? . . . Editors at these magazines deal in different ways with the GenX stereotypes: they hate them, use them, resist them, endlessly analyze them, and, in the best of cases, try to rise above them, to be about something more than just being young." Even decades later, as Gen X approached midlife and their youth was merely a memory, many of the stereotypes that were once only associated with youth remained: cynical, lazy, and, of course, slacker. In their youth, perhaps the most salient Gen X descriptor to emerge was slacker.

While most people believe the term *slacker* has a negative connotation, late Baby Boomer filmmaker Richard Linklater, director of the movie *Slackers*, offers a different perspective. In 1991, Linklater described a slacker as "someone who's being responsible to themselves. It's not avoiding responsibility; it's finding your own path through this maze of programming and pressures" (Gordinier, 23). Linklater noted how many slackers lived in university towns and were highly educated, something that was often overlooked by mainstream media. Not only were "slackers" hypersmart, he argued, but they were also proud of their intelligence (Gordinier, 26). From the outside, it appeared as though slackers were wasting their time; in reality, however, they were learning (Gordinier, 26).

Also defending the generation and against the negative connotation surrounding the word, generational scholar Tom Pace argues that Gen X is a total contradiction, and that the slacker label is utterly undeserved ("Portrait of the Xer"). Others have also argued that Gen Xers as slackers, cynics, and materialistic are all myths perpetuated in movies and other aspects of popular culture (Howe and Strauss, *13th Gen*; Giles and Miller). Additionally, Howe and Strauss argue that these myths were used by other generations to "rekindle a sense of national community—and urgency" (*13th Gen*, 22). In other words, as a collective, Gen X and their slackerdom became a metaphor for what was wrong in America. For both Silents and Baby Boomers, Gen X was the rallying cry for much-needed change in the country.

According to a study by Paula Poindexter and Dominic Lasorsa, Gen X was initially, and overwhelmingly, associated with "young" (33 percent); "slacker" accounted for only 9 percent of the study results. Over time, however, "slacker" became more salient. Many Gen Xers acknowledge, even embrace, the contradictions of their generational portrait, but tend to bristle at the "slacker" label. Writer Cheryl O'Donovan notes:

> Leigh is a 28-year-old technical writer . . . [and] she bristles at the term. "When I hear Generation X, I think of dirty flannel shirts, MTV and Mountain Dew commercials. I'm not a part of that. I know that if I get laid off tomorrow, I have skills to get a new job quickly. . . . [i]f my current position does not provide an opportunity to learn. . . . I will have no problem leaving."

Members of Gen X have simultaneously acknowledged their widely noted cynicism, while also describing themselves as "independent, determined, ambitious, innovative, and politically conscientious, giving the lie to the lazy, listless image of Gen Xers portrayed in the mainstream" (Shugart, 135). As Gozzi notes, the Gen X slacker/cynic stereotype "contains enough truth to be interesting, enough distortion and stereotyping to be infuriating. [Generation Xers] live in the richest nation in the world, are well-educated, and still have tremendous opportunities" (333). Part of the contradiction lies within, as noted by Howe and Strauss, because Gen Xers tend to be "individually optimistic and collectively pessimistic" (Lavin). The duo compares Gen Xers to "a group of skydivers hurtling to the ground with only one parachute among them, but each one expects he'll get it" (Lavin). Herein lies the messy contradiction and paradox that is Gen X.

Despite their distrust in authority and traditional institutions, for example, Gen X can also be remarkably loyal to individual family members and friends, in addition to being incredibly resourceful. For adult Gen Xers, "starting and maintaining a stable family can be a unique source of pride—the pride you get for achieving something your own parents did not" (Howe and Strauss, *Millennials Rising*, 56). While Gen Xers are often leery of institutions like family, they also strive to redefine and restore the integrity of them. While it may be true that obtaining a single-family house is more difficult for Gen Xers than it was for their Silent or Baby Boomer parents, they understand "there are plenty of creative ways to live" (Gozzi, 333). Acknowledging this, Gen X works to define a satisfying lifestyle despite, for example, social and economic factors.

In his study on emerging adults, Jeffrey Arnett notes that there are a variety of reasons why Gen Xers view themselves—and are viewed by others—as pessimistic, but "common responses included limited economic opportunities and increased awareness of societal problems such as crime and environmental destruction" (279). Others have noted Gen X's lack of access to the American Dream (Howe and Strauss, *13th Gen*). Unlike previous generations that grew up believing in the American Dream and the fortitude of the American economy, Gen Xers "recall economic warnings and dirgelike jeremiads dating back to the first time they stayed up to watch news stories about stagflation and gas lines" (Howe and Strauss, *13th Gen*, 98). In addition to economic problems, Gen X also experienced a host of societal problems, all painting a dismal future:

"problematic social conditions, including a soaring divorce rate, high rates of working mothers and latchkey children, ecological disaster, the AIDS epidemic, and so forth" (Ortner, 418). Furthermore, during times of distress, Gen Xers learned that they could not necessarily count on authority figures to help remedy these problems.

Like other researchers, Arnett's study found that Gen Xers continue to be positive about their personal futures "even amidst what they see as a grim world" (284). As such, while Gen X continues to channel the independence and self-reliance they learned as children, they also tend to be suspicious and cynical (Gibson, Greenwood, and Murphy Jr.), remaining "faithful to the self-help spirit of the Reagan Revolution" (Howe and Strauss, *13th Gen*, 99–100). Despite a series of hardships and a subsequent heavy dose of cynicism, Gen X has found success as adults in a variety of different sectors, often as entrepreneurs. In fact, in 1999 Gen X became so widely known for their innovation and entrepreneurial spirit that the *New York Times* dubbed them Generation 1099 (Ellin).

For example, while Millennials are often given credit for the proliferation of new technology in the early aughts, it was entrepreneurial Gen Xers such as Elon Musk of PayPal and Tesla (b. 1971), Sergey Brin and Larry Page of Google (b. 1973), Jack Dorsey of Twitter (b. 1976), and Shawn Fanning of 1999's Napster (b. 1980) that changed the digital landscape forever. These Gen Xers laid the groundwork for Millennials like Mark Zuckerberg, the creator of the social media platform Facebook (Williams). Across the country, Gen Xers have succeeded in a variety of different careers because of their perseverance, including careers in technology, television, film, and music. Given Gen Xers' relationship with popular culture, their success in these sectors is unsurprising.

Walk This Way: Gen X and Popular Culture

According to Paul Taylor of the Pew Research Center, the approximate birth years for Gen X are 1965–80 (38). Different researchers have cited a variety of dates, and adding to the intrigue, Coupland argues that Gen X is more of a sensibility than a particular demographic (Gordinier, 22). With any generation, it is important to note that there are no precise dates. Depending on a variety of different factors, people might identify more with a previous generation (or a later one), particularly those born near the beginning or end of a generation. For example, many of those born in the early 1980s have expressed allegiance to both Gen Xers and Millennials (the generation after Gen X), calling themselves Xennials (D'Souza) and the Catalano Generation, named after the iconic Gen X TV character Jordan Catalano, played by Jared Leto on the ABC network show *My So-Called Life* (Shafrir).

In addition, the Oregon Trail Generation (Garvey), named after a 1970s video game played in classrooms across the country, has also been informally used to describe people born on the latter cusp of Gen X. Those born in this time period have been so widely discussed that many now believe Xennials constitute a microgeneration. According to Ryan W. Miller of *USA Today*, because of their birth years Xennials "experienced world events, and especially technology, in unique ways particular to their age." Their assessment of the world is a combination of Gen X and Millennial values and viewpoints.

The Catalano Generation and Oregon Trail Generation feel appropriate as names, as it has been widely noted that Gen X enjoys popular culture (Hornblower). They grew up with, and in some cases, as with latchkey kids, were raised by popular culture; they bonded over it. Given this intimate relationship with popular culture, Gen X writers, directors, and actors boast impressive achievements in the industry. It is no surprise that their achievements—in music, movies, and television—often reflect the attitudes of their generation. Some examples include the grunge movement (a descriptor used not by the musicians themselves, but by mainstream media) in music and movies like *Reality Bites* and *Clerks*. Helene Shugart, critical cultural scholar, argues that music and film of this time period gave "rise to distinct genres that accurately represent and reflect the rhetorical and aesthetic dimensions of Generation X" (137). Works produced by Gen Xers, even across media, had/have a similar aesthetic feel.

One of Gen X's greatest contributions to pop culture is the grunge music movement, "which is all about glorifying marginalization and alienation" (Shafrir). Bands like Nirvana, Pearl Jam, and Soundgarden, staples of the movement, were often cited for their raw and honest lyrics. These bands were rough-around-the-edges and flawed, making them the embodiment of Gen X and the antithesis of eighties excess—the make-up, the hair, the endless party, and the obsession with image. Along with other pop culture artifacts of the time, the bands not only reflected Gen X values but also helped Gen Xers bond with one another over popular culture in ways previous generations had not (Pace, "Portrait of the Xer"). Similarly, also addressing marginalization and alienation, the rise of hip hop during this time period also produced raw lyrics that documented the lives of Gen Xers, namely Gen Xers of color. Artists such as Public Enemy, Ice Cube, and A Tribe Called Quest not only changed the music industry but also introduced their plight to suburban white males, a demographic who were large consumers of rap music.

This book is a close study of Gen X's popular culture, namely popular culture of the 1980s featuring coming-of-age Gen Xers. Throughout these pages, I explore the parallels between iconic 1980s popular culture, namely film, and the first three seasons of the Netflix series *Stranger Things*, which is set in the 1980s, moving beyond the widely noted (at times non sequitur) 1980s Easter eggs (hidden or unexplained references or objects) to a common underlying narrative. Throughout the book, I aim to demonstrate how *Stranger Things* draws on 1980s popular culture to pay tribute to—and occasionally challenge—Gen X's cynical and evolving outlook on three key interwoven American institutions: family, economy, and government. The representation of these values is what makes the series a slice of nostalgia and quintessentially Gen X.

It's Tricky: A Sociocultural Approach to Genre Analysis

This book is a work of criticism. My main analytical method uses genre analysis to describe the representation of Gen X in 1980s films featuring children and teenagers and explore the degree to which *Stranger Things* does so, paying homage to Gen X. *Genre* is a French word meaning type or kind and has been used to describe categories of movies, television series, and books. Genres do not emerge from an isolated text; they emerge "from the intertextual relations between multiple texts, resulting in a common category" (Mittell, 6). A genre analysis considers patterns, trends, and motifs across a body of programming, embedded in our cultural practices, which share commonalities (Shary). The classification of texts is a "fundamental aspect of the way texts of all kinds are understood," not only by theorists but also by audiences (Neale, 3). Ultimately, it is the audience who brings texts together, thus making genre inherently intertextual (Mittell, 6).

In previous years, genre theorists have focused on defining ideal types of genres and have often used these venerated types to evaluate other texts (Feuer, 139). This approach is likely because of the methodology's roots in literary criticism. Literary generic categories are often broad and, due to a variety of factors, are less likely to evolve rapidly. By contrast, television and film generic categories tend to be "culturally specific and temporally limited" (Feuer, 140). Because of this difference, as genre theory began to emerge as a methodology in film studies, many researchers argued for a more *social* method of studying genres, noting how important it is to acknowledge and carefully examine the fluid social context in which these genres are produced.

A social generic approach to both film and television criticism seeks to understand how film (or television) represents individuals or groups of people with the understanding that these artifacts "are both aesthetic and cultural documents produced by an industry whose aim is to appeal to (often larger) populations" (Shary, 11). It is from this perspective I approach the texts in this study. By using a social approach, genre is not seen as fixed and inherent within any given text or artifact; rather, genre is fluid and part of a larger cultural context. There is no desire to find and define the ideal 1980s teenage pop culture film or series. Rather, I seek to analyze how the dataset represents Gen Xers and how these representations are shaped by Gen Xers. As Barry Keith Grant, literary and film scholar, argues, genres are "cultural myths serving similar social and ideological functions in that they tend to take social debates and tensions and cast them into formulaic narratives, condensing them into dramatic conflicts" (4). This, in turn, can help audiences make sense of the "abstract social forces that effect our lives" (Grant, 4). A primary goal of my analysis is to understand how the texts in this study, all set in the 1980s and featuring children or teenagers, represent Gen X's experiences and attitudes toward a variety of institutions—and how these representations compare to representations in *Stranger Things*.

For this study, I analyze the top movies of the 1980s as determined by Internet Movie Database (IMDb) users as of July 2018, ranked according to "number of votes." Because the full list includes over 30,000 titles, I analyze only those films which (1) are in the top 50, (2) prominently feature teenagers and young adults, and (3) received a rating of at least seven stars. These criteria result in a film list that acknowledges the collaborative, collective intelligence of the audience—as opposed to "expert" reviewers—to define "good" movies (MacNamara), while also noting the social potency of widely viewed popular culture artifacts. Furthermore, my film list features characters and motifs drawn upon throughout *Stranger Things*. Taking these criteria and considerations into account, the films chosen for analysis (from least popular to most popular) are:

Gremlins
Big
Nightmare on Elm Street
The Goonies
Ferris Bueller's Day Off
The Breakfast Club
Stand by Me
E.T. the Extra Terrestrial
Dead Poets Society
Back to the Future II
Back to the Future[1]

You're the Inspiration: Gen X and *Stranger Things*

As a series, *Stranger Things* is a product of two borderline Gen Xers (Xennials) who overtly pay homage to their generation and the decade in which they were raised.² As borderline Gen Xers, brothers Matt and Ross Duffer learned a lot about the 1980s via popular culture. In that regard, their work is a representation of the representations of the 1980s. It is then no surprise that *Stranger Things* is filled with references to 1980s television and film. *Stranger Things* gives aesthetic nods to Steven Spielberg and Stephen King, heavy hitters of that time period; and as *CBS Sunday Morning* notes, the series reflects the Duffer brothers' favorite films growing up: '80s sci-fi and horror that reflected the suburbia and friendships they recognized and found familiar ("'Stranger Things' to Once Again Go Bump in the Night").

Season One of *Stranger Things* opens with four young boys playing Dungeons & Dragons, the board game that became popular in the 1980s. After a ten-hour marathon game, one of the boys, Will, goes missing. Throughout the rest of the season, friends search for Will with help from a mysterious girl they meet named Eleven. As the search intensifies, 1980s popular culture artifacts appear throughout. At least to some extent, the boys' journey in Season One parallels the quests of the teenage boys in *Stand by Me* (searching for a missing local boy "who went out to pick blueberries and no one saw him since") and *The Goonies* (searching for pirate treasure to save their family home). According to IGN writer Eric Goldman, "If you were a kid of the 1980s, or if you simply are a fan of the films of the 1980s, Netflix's new series *Stranger Things* will feel very familiar in very satisfying ways. . . . The depiction of these young kids and the way they speak, interact and, yep, ride bikes together, feels incredibly Spielbergian...." The bike riding (*E.T.*), the walk along the train tracks (*Stand by Me*—minus the near-death-by-train experience), the bond among friends (*The Goonies*), and the adventure are all aesthetically consistent, prompting a critic from *Time* to argue that the series's "fondness for its own source material makes its nostalgia warm and inclusive" (D'Addario).

Since the release of Season One in 2016, *Stranger Things* has captivated and delighted both casual audiences and popular culture scholars, resulting in a plethora of articles written on the series. In particular, scholars have studied a variety of aspects related to representation, specifically representation related to family and gender. For instance, in regard to familial representation, scholars have studied mothers adhering to, and breaking, traditional gender role stereotypes (Carruthers; Boudreau), parental authority (Baker and Howell), and the nuclear family (Franklin). Additionally, there have been several queer readings of the series that have allowed scholars to investigate and contest the categorization of gender and sexuality in the series. For instance, Heather Freeman argues that *Stranger Things* succumbs to heteropatriarchal narrative paradigms. She notes how Barb, a possible queer character, is quickly "flattened by quick victimhood" in Season One, while Steve, the archetypal, heteronormative bad boy, is portrayed sympathetically throughout the series (Freeman, 99). Based on her analysis, Freeman believes *Stranger Things* is an example of "comfort nostalgia," a form of nostalgia that "risks being fully *self*-reflexive, rather than *other*-oriented, complacent rather than galvanizing" (93).

Given the setting and the numerous popular media articles dedicated to discussing it, it should come as no surprise that different aspects of nostalgia are one of the areas receiving a significant amount of scholarly attention, particularly because of the intertextual nature of the series. According to media scholar Tracey Mollet, the first two seasons of the series meld film, television, literature, and geek culture into one artifact: "This is done both within the text itself, and through the audience's invited interaction with the text, as the show demonstrates significant awareness of the trans-medial, Easter-egg hunting tendencies of its binge-watching followers." Throughout the series, the Duffer brothers use optional intertextuality, in which audiences, based on their knowledge, may or may not find connections to other texts.

According to Aja Romano, critic and writer for *Vox*, in Season Three, the final episode offers one great big nod to nerd culture, as Suzie and Dustin sing the theme song from the fantasy nerd flick *The Neverending Story*: "This scene, in which Dustin and Suzie sing the duet together, is a literal love song to everything *Stranger Things* represents to its fans: a love of the 1980s, of geek culture and fantasy, of childhood whimsy, and above all, of friendships" (Romano). This is one example of the type of intertextuality used by the brothers to pay homage to iconic 1980s popular culture. Despite this reference, those with limited intertextual knowledge can still enjoy the series. One does not have to know the movie *The Neverending Story* to be touched by the scene. Ultimately, and to the delight of many Gen Xers, there are many moments like this throughout the series, as audiences are rewarded for their intertextual knowledge (Jenkins).

Stranger Things is a text that Gen X audiences appreciate, in part because they were raised on intertextual TV and pop culture. Gen X is a generation that welcomes allusions not only to Spielberg and company, but also to Dungeons & Dragons. They welcome Dustin's repeated references to Lando from *The*

Empire Strikes Back, Eleven levitating the *Millennium Falcon*, and the children watching *He-Man*. They enjoy seeing Mike and his friends dressing up as characters from *Ghostbusters* for Halloween. In his article "Nostalgic Things: *Stranger Things* and the Pervasiveness of Nostalgic Television," Joseph Sirianni examines how various textual elements (e.g., narration, setting, decor, props, costumes, music, characters) of the past are used to transport viewers to a different time and elicit specific emotional responses from them. Sirianni notes how "trapper keepers, cans of pudding, walkie talkies, radio boomboxes, Rubik's cube, white wicker bedroom furniture, movie and music posters, wood paneling, ruffled blouses, and corded telephones" were used as period markers of the 1980s (192–93). In this book, however, I argue that it is also important to look beyond aesthetics to other aspects of the series.

It is critical to note that *Stranger Things* reflects not only the popular culture of the 1980s but also many of the attitudes prevalent during the decade. It is here I focus my attention. As the fabric of American culture changed during the formative years of Gen X, as noted earlier in the chapter, many felt "unwanted or even betrayed by the institutions that comprise the bedrock of existence in the United States" (Hanson, 168). Gen Xers grew up cynical about the "powerlessness of elders" (Howe and Strauss, *13th Gen*, 52). According to Howe and Strauss, "When they reached adolescence, national confidence weakened, and community and family life splintered" (*13th Gen*, 52). Having seen corruption in "families, churches, the government," Gen X likes popular culture that pokes fun of the establishment (Owen, 10). It is no surprise, then, that in addition to its source material, the series explores Gen X's complicated relationship with American institutions, including family, the government, and the economy. While 1980s-aesthetic popular culture Easter eggs are what catch the attention of most viewers, as popular media articles and reviews suggest, the Easter eggs are not the only reason why the series is a slice of nostalgia for those watching. What makes the series unique, and middle-aged Gen X audiences able to connect to it, is the way in which it embodies the interests, skills, and values of those coming of age in the 1980s, those part of Gen X.

Here and Now: It Only Gets Stranger from Here

In this book, I start by sharing research on Gen X's perception of family, particularly how adolescent and teenage Gen Xers perceived the 1980s sprawl to suburbia, the rising divorce rates, their latchkey status, and the literal or figurative unraveling of their nuclear families. During their familial turmoil, Gen Xers often turned to peers, popular culture, and other trusted adults, such as teachers, for support and guidance. Throughout chapter 2, I demonstrate how *Stranger Things* embodies these uniquely Gen X experiences. I show how the series illustrates Gen X's expanding definitions of family and home, noting how the series both parallels, and occasionally diverges from, the 1980s dataset.

In chapter 3, I turn my attention to another institution, one so intertwined with each and every American family: the economy. I begin by describing how the economic landscape of the 1980s heavily influenced the family dynamics discussed in chapter 2. I pay particular attention to the widening income gap that increased dramatically during this time period and discuss how this gap paradoxically gave rise to conspicuous consumption, in which Gen X actively participated. Despite real concerns on how consumption, particularly mindless consumption, can lead to the loss of community and culture health, chapter three outlines how Gen X helped give rise to the materialism that would later come to define the 1980s. I conclude this chapter by documenting how access to the American Dream—or lack thereof—is addressed in 1980s popular culture and *Stranger Things*. My analysis shows that the tumultuous economic climate of the 1980s led to increased cynicism in Gen Xers, and that this cynicism was ultimately reflected on large and small screens. Despite this representation, the 1980s dataset fails to explore the relationship between economic power and social and political power—whereas *Stranger Things* addresses it more implicitly.

In chapter 4, I describe Gen X's relationship with two additional key institutions: the political and legal systems. I begin by describing Gen X's relationship with both local and national law enforcement and government officials, outlining how these relationships are represented in 1980s popular culture. Throughout their lifetime, Gen Xers have been given ample reasons to be suspicious of the government and its agents. Because of these reasons, a common motif found in iconic 1980s popular culture is the bumbling or uncooperative police officer. To some extent, this motif is also seen in *Stranger Things* with some slight variations. Throughout both 1980s popular culture and the series, we see unhelpful local and national authorities, many of which are unwilling to oblige Gen Xers seeking assistance. In many instances, they only listen when the situation is dire or too late. These representations serve two purposes: they highlight Gen X's institutional cynicism and reinforce it.

Throughout this book, my analysis demonstrates how the Duffer brothers chose to stay close to their source material, iconic films of the 1980s, much to the delight of their audiences. There are only a few times in which the series diverges from the 1980s dataset, and I believe these times are worth close examination. In chapter 5, I explore the times in which the series deviates, focusing on what has happened to Gen X since the dataset was released. For example, I discuss why stereotypes persist despite Gen X serving as productive members of society for decades, often working directly against these stereotypes. I examine whether or not these stereotypes, and what has happened to Gen X since the dataset was released, can help explain the differences between the texts. Gen X's midlife experiences, just as the experiences of their youth, are both generated and articulated in popular culture, including *Stranger Things*. While the series reflects Gen X's perception of key American institutions, it also reflects Gen X's growth and evolving thoughts on family, the economy, and the government.

It has been widely noted how *Stranger Things* is a 1980s nostalgia trip for its viewers because of how the series uses aesthetics and popular culture to accurately recreate the decade. In this book, I look beyond the overt references to 1980s popular culture and the 1980s popular culture Easter eggs sprinkled throughout and focus on how the series represents the *attitudes* of children and teenagers of the time: coming-of-age (and then middle-aged) Gen Xers. I believe it is this aspect of the series, not the Easter eggs, that makes *Stranger Things* a trip back in time for viewers—and quintessentially Gen X. I believe documenting the attitudes toward key American institutions is how the series parallels 1980s iconic films featuring teenagers and children. Throughout the series, the Duffer brothers clearly capture what is was like to be part of the "middle child" generation. Enjoy this deep examination of how *Stranger Things* is a homage to Gen X, and take note: It only gets stranger from here!

—— 2 ——
What's Love Got to Do with It?
Gen X and the Family Unit

Ronald Reagan's election ushered in a period characterized by individualistic pursuits and, at the same time, economic uncertainty. This resulted in a myriad of problems for coming-of-age Gen Xers, not the least of which was family. For example, parents spent less time with their children because a) both parents were active in the workforce, b) one or more parents sought individual gratification outside the family, or c) parents split custody of their children due to divorce. Howe and Strauss note that many Gen Xers, as children, "felt more like castaways, avoided by adults more interested at that time in rediscovering themselves" (*Millennials Rising*, 44). In other cases, the family dynamic became toxic *because* parents remained married and personally unfulfilled.

Generating and reinforcing Gen X's cynical appraisal of the nuclear family, popular culture of the time reflected these new dynamics, critiquing Reagan's conservative social policies and exploring the "horror" within the family unit (Butler, 75). During this time, parenting became more egalitarian. For many families during the 1980s, adults became more childlike, and children became more adultlike (Howe and Strauss, *13th Gen*, 62). Because children in the 1980s were often alone, adults "removed shields that previously had protected children from the harsh truths of life" (Howe and Strauss, *13th Gen*, 66). Children were lectured on how to protect themselves and given books that taught them how to deal with adult problems. As such, it is said that Gen X learned to be more independent than previous generations. Unreliable familial figures also led Gen Xers to look for belonging outside the traditional family unit: "because Gen Xers, speaking in the most general terms, aren't tethered to family and other institutions in the ways that their predecessors were, they create a comforting cocoon of artifice" (Hanson, 43). Even for Gen Xers from two-parent households, the notion of family was expanded. For example, throughout *Stranger Things*, Eleven uses the frame of "home" to explore and define family. At various times, her dependable friends, a "sister" from similar circumstances, popular culture, and a pseudo-step-dad all embody "home" for Eleven, but at no time does home resemble the traditional nuclear family. In fact, her blood relatives actually prove problematic. In this chapter, I explore numerous interrelated concepts associated with family, including the concept of "home," tension between parental expectations and expectations of parents, and Gen X's substitutes for parental bonds. I begin, however, by discussing representations of the family unit.

We're a Happy Family: Representations of Traditional and Nontraditional Families

Stranger Things is "part descendant of and part homage to genre films of the 1980s" (Morton, 94). As such, *Stranger Things* and the 1980s popular culture the show draws upon reflect the changing American family of the 1980s. These texts represent several traditional "nuclear" families in various states of health as well as single-parent households, which increased in the 1980s due to rising divorce rates. According to the Pew Research Center, "In 1960, the height of the post-World War II baby boom, there was one dominant family form. At that time 73% of all children were living in a family with two married parents in their first marriage. By 1980, 61% of children were living in this type of family . . ." ("Parenting in America"). The texts analyzed do not romanticize the nuclear family of the 1960s; in fact, *Dead Poets Society* and *Stand by Me* explicitly critique such period romanticizations, suggesting that these romanticized representations are shallow and flawed. Texts in this study repeatedly show all types of families burdened with both interpersonal and financial problems.

The Traditional Nuclear Family

One of the more salient themes to emerge from the 1980s dataset is that of the tarnished nuclear family. Indeed, many of the problems facing children in 1980s popular culture are directly or indirectly related to their family life, and the films during this time period seem determined to strip the veneer of perfection from this particular institution. For example, as noted by Shirley R. Steinberg and Joe L. Kincheloe regarding *The Breakfast Club*, "Every action of the five teens is driven by a negative interaction in the home" (118). Each character, in some capacity, is in detention as a "direct result of familial dysfunction" (Steinberg and Kincheloe, 119).

Familial dysfunction takes on many forms in all of the texts. For example, in *Stand by Me* three of the four children come from families with significant problems, ranging from abuse to disparagement. In *Ferris Bueller's Day Off*, Lawrence Grossberg notes that family is the "site of struggle (with a jealous sister) and manipulation (the film opens with Ferris giving the audience advice about how to manipulate parents)" (87). Ferris acknowledges that he "used to think that my family was the only one that had weirdness in it," but admits that all families have their issues—including his best friend Cameron's, whose parents hate each other but remain married (*Ferris Bueller's Day Off*).

Another manifestation of the tarnished nuclear family is violence. In *Stand by Me*, Teddy and Chris have fathers who, while present, are violent. Teddy's father was sent away for burning Teddy's ear on a stove, a memory Teddy is forced to confront when an older man warns Teddy that he will end up like his father. Chris's father is an alcoholic. The profound effect of growing up in dysfunctional families, particularly *violent* dysfunctional families, was not lost on the narrator, an adult Gordie. Speaking about Chris, he states: "He came from a bad family. And everyone just knew he'd turn out bad. Including Chris" (*Stand by Me*). In this study, the list of characters impacted by violence is extensive. In *Back to the Future II*, Future-Biff is violent with both fists and firearms. Neil Perry's father in *Dead Poets Society* belittles, controls, and yells. In *The Breakfast Club*, when talking about his home life with peer Andrew, Bender recreates a powerful scene, in which his father abuses him emotionally and physically:

> (Dad): "Stupid, worthless, no-good, god damn freeloadin' son of a bitch, retarded, big mouth, know-it-all asshole, jerk."
> Bender: [in a child's voice] "You forgot ugly, crazy, and disrespectful."

(Dad): [backhands child] "SHUT UP BITCH! Go fix me a
   turkey pot pie."
Bender: "What about you, dad?"
(Dad) "Fuck you."
Bender: "Whoa, dad what about you?"
(Dad) "FUCK YOU!"
Bender: "NO, DAD, WHAT ABOUT YOU?"
(Dad) "FUCK. YOU." [mimics a punch]

During this explosive exchange, Andrew is skeptical of Bender's
story, arguing it is all likely for show, part of Bender's pro-
jected "tough guy" image. After Andrew expresses doubt,
however, Bender pulls up his sleeve and shows Andrew poof
of his abuse—a cigar burn on his arm, a punishment for spilled
paint in the garage.

   Finally, various characters and scenes throughout these
films depict a common concern for Gen X children: their
"nuclear" parents are more interested in taking care of
themselves than engaging with their children. Ferris's friend
Cameron has a mom who constantly travels to escape the
museum-like quality of their home (beautiful, cold, and
no touching). Parents who cannot physically depart their
surroundings use liquor as a source of diversion. Lorraine,
Marty's mom in *Back to the Future*, escapes domestic dol-
drums with copious amounts of vodka. Gordie, the main
character in *Stand by Me*, who also comes from a nuclear family, says very early in the movie, "That summer at home, I had
become the invisible boy." Similarly, despite being from very
different families fraught by very different problems, both
Gordie and Allison (*The Breakfast Club*) feel their parents
ignore them on the basis that they wish they were different
or "better." For example, after the death of Gordie's brother,

his grief-stricken parents continually ask him, "Why can't you have friends like Denny?" (*Stand by Me*).

Similarly, we can infer from Lorraine's drinking in *Back to the Future*, and corresponding work uniforms worn by two of her children, that she is dissatisfied not only with her inattentive husband but her children's level of success. In *The Breakfast Club*, despite outward differences, characters Claire, Bender, and Allison also echo this concern. Bender asserts, "I could disappear forever, and it wouldn't make a difference," while Allison describes her home life as unbearable because her parents ignore her (*The Breakfast Club*). Throughout the texts analyzed, this is a common theme: wishing for a "perfect" nuclear family, but knowing it is impossible to achieve.

In *Stranger Things*, two of the children's families are nuclear: Lucas and Mike. We rarely see Lucas's family, but by all outward appearances, he has a relatively stable home life with a supportive mom, a present father who converses while reading the paper at family breakfast, and a sister who won't stay out of his room. Mike's family, on the other hand, embodies many of the toxic nuclear family traits found in the 1980s popular culture upon which the show draws. Mike's family—like the Buellers, the Perrys in *Dead Poets Society*, or Nancy's family in *Nightmare on Elm Street*—appears "normal": the siblings tease one another, mom and dad are still married, they own a home in one of Hawkins's "nicer" neighborhoods, and the family still eats together. It is the very portrait of suburban harmony.

We soon notice cracks in the façade of perfection. Upon closer inspection, Mike's dad is more or less detached from his family—another indicator that "nuclear" is not necessarily authentic or perfect. Nancy, Mike's sister, explicitly lays out her family's dysfunction for viewers in a conversation with Jonathan in Season One: "I don't think my parents ever loved

each other. My mom was young. My dad was older, but he had
a cushy job, money, came from a good family. So they bought
a nice house at the end of a cul-de-sac and started their *nuclear
family*" ("Chapter Five: The Flea and the Acrobat"). Nancy puts
a cynical, mocking emphasis on the word nuclear, confirming
what some viewers suspected all along.

As noted by Elsa M. Carruthers, Mike and Nancy's mother,
Karen, appears to be a good mother, but she is unaware of what
is going on in her own home, including Eleven living in her
basement in Season One. In Season One, when Karen visits
Joyce after Will's disappearance, she gives Joyce a casserole, a
seemingly nice gesture, but as Carruthers observes, ". . . she
really isn't there to help, but to see how far Joyce is fallen"
(132). Karen mitigates her own unhappiness by reveling in the
struggle of others. In Season Two, Karen becomes even more
detached from her family. A glass of wine is omnipresent, and
Ted's lack of attention (to phones, doorbells, and presumably
to her) becomes increasingly frustrating to Karen, and it is clear
she wishes for more.

Karen's level of detachment culminates in a scene in which
she is taking a bath, reading a romance novel, and sipping wine.
The doorbell rings twice. She yells at Ted, who is napping in a
chair, to get the door. Annoyed at her husband's nonresponse,
she answers the door and finds Billy—the newly relocated
town bad boy—looking for his sister. In Season Three, Karen
is once again tempted by Billy, coming even closer to infidelity,
as she agrees to a rendezvous with him, now a lifeguard, after
he offers her private "swimming lessons" ("Chapter One: Suzie,
Do You Copy?"). While Karen ultimately does not meet Billy
as planned at the local motel (she sees Ted sleeping in his chair
with their youngest daughter and feels guilty), her annoyance
and disdain for her husband continues, and it is clear the sexual

tension between her and Billy is real. It is in these moments that the audience sees just how tarnished Mike's family actually is.

This leads viewers to a central tension present within the texts: should I stay or should I go? In Season One, it is perhaps appropriate that Jonathan and Will bond over the Clash song of the same name, because many Gen X families—real and fictional—struggled with the question of staying together or splitting up. Staying together may have been easier, financially beneficial, or simply the "normal" thing to do to keep up appearances. But what if the family and children are better off with one parent? It is hard to argue that the Perrys in *Dead Poets Society* would not have been happier without dad around. The 1980s texts analyzed here are universally critical of the nuclear family, but the *ideal* of the nuclear family—at least in its normative construction—is still taken for granted. In 1980s America, despite its flaws, the nuclear family is still something for which to strive.

Back to the Future also serves as an example. After traveling back in time, Marty returns to the "perfect" family: George and Lorraine are happily married, as George followed his dream of becoming an author. His siblings are successful, and the family home is upper-middle-class and tastefully decorated. There are other visual markers of success, including a new truck for Marty and a BMW for his dad. It appears that despite the dripping cynicism surrounding nuclear families, the nuclear family is still revered. It remains the ideal that one should aim to have, to achieve.

Recent scholarship notes how Gen Xers fear passing dysfunction onto their children. Gen Xers who maintain a stable nuclear family feel "a unique source of pride—the pride you get for achieving something your parents did not" (Howe and Strauss, *Millennials Rising*, 56). Various authors note that representations of the "perfect," nuclear, suburban family fail to address various lived realities in suburbia: conspicuous consumption, racism, and the above-mentioned family dynamics (Franklin, 176; Smith, 217). As the next section demonstrates, the uprightness of nontraditional families, and of single parentage in particular, represents an area where *Stranger Things* breaks the representational mold.

The Nontraditional Family

Within the 1980s dataset, representations of remarried or divorced families are scant. Future-Lorraine married an abusive and power-tripping version of Biff in *Back to the Future II* because George, her first husband, died, and we briefly see the equally unhealthy union between Billy's father and Max's mother in the second season of *Stranger Things*. Among single-parent households, the most present aspect, at least among the films examined, remains the absence of representation. Mary, Elliott's mom in *E.T. the Extra-Terrestrial*, is the only significant manifestation of single parentage among the movies sampled. She lives in an upper-class neighborhood with her three children; her husband, from whom she is separated, is "in Mexico with Sally" (*E.T. the Extra-Terrestrial*). Mary's occasional outburst toward her estranged husband indicates that the relationship has taken a great toll on her. Steven Spielberg's treatment of Mary's family captures the struggle and emotion of single parentage, but there is no sense of valorization. The representation of nontraditional families is just as broken as nuclear ones; in fact, both types of families struggle with some of the same problems, such as parental disengagement from children—albeit for different reasons.

Conversely, *Stranger Things* simultaneously echoes and challenges our conception of "broken" single parent homes. In Season Two, we learn that Dustin is the product of a single-parent household, and the relationship between him and his mother appears unhealthy. Because his mother clearly struggles with the impact of abandonment and possibly divorce, she treats Dustin like she would a husband; she treats him like the man of the house. (Her exact situation is never explicitly defined.) As noted by Ashley Carranza, Mrs. Henderson relies on Dustin for companionship and to "stabilize her own state of mind" (13). Her behavior creates a dangerous level of co-dependency, eroding any sort of stable parent-child relationship. There are moments when Dustin is in clear need of parenting, and it appears as though his mother knows it. Yet, Mrs. Henderson is unable to give him the support and type of attention he needs, given her own mental health issues. In the first episode of Season Three, however, Dustin is seen returning from camp, suggesting that Mrs. Henderson is perhaps in a better state of mind, as she allowed Dustin to leave for part of the summer. This is unverifiable, however, as she is absent from the rest of the season.

Additionally, Sheriff Jim Hopper's figurative (and later literal) adoption of Eleven in Season Two plays out via familiar themes of conflict and violence. Before elaborating on Hopper and Eleven's relationship, however, I examine the ways in which the Byers family—Joyce, Jonathan, and Will—add to the discourse on nontraditional families. Through the Byers, previous representations of single parentage are challenged, suggesting that single-parent households can be a better environment than two-parent households.

Stranger Things plays with our definition of "perfect" families by aesthetically juxtaposing the Byers and Wheeler (Ted, Karen, Nancy, and Mike) families, and the contrast is astounding. In the opening episode of the series, as Joyce and Jonathan search frantically for her car keys, and then for Will, Mike's family comfortably and calmly enjoys breakfast in the Wheeler home. Throughout the first two seasons, the Byers home is dark, unkempt, and in disrepair; it has a worn, lived-in look. In contrast, the Wheeler home is always bright, tidy, and well-maintained. This is yet another vehicle by which *Stranger Things* critiques the "outward perfection" of the nuclear Wheelers by contrasting them with both the "outward turmoil" and (more importantly) the "genuine interactions" of the Byers family (Franklin, 179–80).

Stranger Things also contrasts Karen and Joyce as parents. Both Karen and Joyce work, but while Karen (and her ever-present glass of wine) seems to cope with parenting, Joyce tortures herself for not being a better, more present and available parent. Superficially, Karen embodies the caring parent who is home by five and available to talk with her kids, while Joyce is the absent single parent working extra shifts to make ends meet. Beneath the surface, however, we see two vastly different levels of commitment to their children. As Franklin argues, the "structurally weaker [family] supported by a single parent comes to represent a family structure that may be considered superior to that of tradition," a family whose "richness" comes not from material possessions but genuine interaction (179–80). In Season Three, Joyce draws attention to their maternal differences when she asks Karen if she has seen the children. Karen replies nonchalantly, "I can hardly keep track these days. You know how it is—summer!" ("Chapter Seven: The Bite"). Whereas Joyce is beside herself with worry, Karen is more interested in enjoying herself at the fair, as she slips a five-dollar bill to a carnival worker to ensure she has the best view of the upcoming Fourth of July fireworks.

This is not to say the Byers are perfect. In the scene above, for example, Joyce was out of town with Hopper, solving the mystery of her demagnetized magnets. (During this time, her children were not a priority.) It would also be remiss not to acknowledge that Will's latchkey status in Season One had serious consequences; it sets the entire series in motion. Before Will goes missing, he runs home, scared, and his mom is nowhere to be found. Because he is alone, he is easily sucked into the Upside Down world by his worst fear: a monster he and his friends call the Demogorgon. It takes Joyce and Jonathan time to realize Will is even missing. Jonathan is busy fulfilling many "parental" roles such as cooking breakfast while Joyce rushes around getting ready for work. Joyce and Jonathan soon discover that neither can confirm whether Will came home the previous evening because Jonathan took extra shifts to make extra money for the family—yet another parental role placed upon him. This makes Joyce even more upset because Jonathan was supposed to be home to greet Will. At the episode's end, Joyce feels bad for not being there for Jonathan, and Jonathan feels bad not being there for Will ("Chapter One: The Vanishing of Will Byers").

Upon the apparent discovery of Will floating dead in the river, Karen comforts her son Mike, while Jonathan assumes a more adult role and comforts Joyce ("Chapter Three: Holly Jolly"). Relationships like Joyce and Jonathan's were increasingly common in the 1980s, as children were forced to "parent" adults. Carranza notes: "As adults take on roles that conflict with home responsibilities, they share the responsibilities of rearing with their children" (15). Particularly in single-parent households, the tough economy that afflicted the 1980s strained familial relationships, much like the Byers family, a topic I further explore in chapter 3. Gen Xers like Jonathan, because of their upbringing, were forced to take on adult responsibilities and master self-reliance (O'Donovan, 17).

Even though the Byers family is a single-parent household for the duration of the series, and Joyce is constructed as an unstable, fringe resident of Hawkins vis-à-vis the more mainstream folks, they feel the most honest throughout the series. While they may be considered broken by traditional definitions of nuclear families, they are real. In Season Two, however, the Byers family dynamic changes a bit as Joyce starts dating Bob. Joyce is initially smitten, yet leery. Throughout their courtship, viewers see Joyce revert to teenage antics, including making out with Bob in a supply closet at work.

Despite Joyce's shortcomings and sometimes immature behavior, she continues to be there for Will, daring to "believe in the supernatural and act on that belief in her radically intuitive and adaptive approaches to parenting" (Baker and Howell). Once again her behavior separates her from the other mothers of Hawkins, as her commitment to her children is clearly unwavering. Additionally, her response to Will's predicament can also be contrasted with Bob's. Bob's response echoes a more traditional "masculine" approach, as he believes Will should simply stand up to the monster (or what Bob believes, at least at the start, are Will's imaginary fears).

It is also worth noting how Bob represents the "normal," functional savior who will deliver Joyce and her family from their dysfunction by bringing them nearer to the nuclear ideal. Indeed, Bob is about as "normal" or "steady" a character as one could write: he manages a Radio Shack, is middle-aged, a little paunchy, a little geeky, has an out-of-touch sense of humor, but most importantly, very much wants to be a dad to Jonathan and Will. Eventually Bob suggests moving the family to Maine where he can provide for them and give them a new life, providing patriarchal salvation. Joyce explains that her family is just "not a normal family," to which Bob replies, "It could be"

("Chapter Two: Trick or Treat, Freak"). In a later episode, Joyce warms to the idea of moving ("Chapter Six: The Spy"). However, as Bob helps Will overcome the shadow monster, he exchanges the role of patriarchal savior for sacrificial lamb. Bob's death—heroic though it is—symbolically demonstrates that the "perfect" family does not exist and further critiques the very idea of nuclear perfection. Despite this aesthetic contrast, the portrait of the middle-class nuclear family in suburbia is bleak.

In sum, the Wheeler/Byers, Karen/Joyce binary is one vehicle *Stranger Things* uses to question nuclear perfection and explore alternative family models. Yet representations of broken single families remind viewers that all families have their problems. In the next section, I explore another way the show broadens the definition of family. In Season Two, Eleven begins a very personal journey, as she searches for her "home."

Our House: Making a House a Home

The concept of home appears occasionally in the 1980s dataset of films. For example, *The Goonies* storyline revolves around saving a family's physical home from developers interested in obtaining and demolishing the house to build a country club. The house serves as a home for main character Mikey, his brother Brand, and his parents. In addition to providing a sanctuary for the traditional family, the house also serves as a sanctuary for Mikey and his friends, who call themselves the goonies. Other films indulge the home-as-sanctuary theme. At the end of *Big*, Josh must decide whether to stay an adult or return to being a child. After little debate, Josh chooses to finish his childhood at "home." Josh asks Susan, his adult love interest, if she, hypothetically, would go back home. She vehemently says no, suggesting that revisiting childhood, and one's childhood home, is not for everyone. Many of the characters and scenarios noted above support the notion that "home" is not a universally positive construct.

Among 1980s films, "home" is most salient in *E.T. the Extra-Terrestrial*. The similarities between the first season of *Stranger Things* and *E.T.* have been widely noted, so it is perhaps not surprising that the search for home becomes Eleven's primary quest in Season Two. Eleven uses the concept of "home" to explore and define family and, like E.T., is only able to go home with the assistance of a loving, yet nontraditional family. This suggests, first, that family—despite all its faults—is still important; and second, as Franklin notes, that definitions of family and home are fluid, "not something bound by blood but rather . . . found through acceptance of the individual" (178). In this section, I review Eleven's quest for home. Her search begins and ends with Sheriff Hopper and is interspersed with both biological and other figurative representations of family and home. Eleven's journey both reinforces and challenges our understanding of Gen X family life.

Father Figure: Eleven and Jim, Part One

In Season One of *Stranger Things*, Eleven's home is Hawkins National Laboratory, under the care of "Papa." Like other father figures in *Stranger Things*, Papa is flawed; he treats Eleven as his "prized pony when she does his bidding, and a criminal when she does not," while offering no love, support, or other things one would expect from a well-functioning father figure (Carruthers, 133). Franklin argues that, upon entering the Wheeler house, Eleven realizes how far detached her home life has been from the societal definition of normal (176–77). However, it is not until Season Two that Eleven's search for home begins in earnest, a search that begins and ends with Hopper.

When we first encounter the duo, Hopper has assumed the role of single pseudo-father, while Eleven embodies an extreme latchkey kid. Hopper instructs Eleven to eat dinner before dessert and teaches her proper expressions of time (eight fifteen as opposed to eight one five). We also see that Hopper's home has rules. These symbols are likely familiar to those who came of age in the 1980s, especially latchkey kids who stayed home while parent(s) worked: the "secret knock" to let Eleven know it is safe to open the door, tightly drawn curtains, and a strict rule to never go out alone, especially during the day ("Chapter One: MADMAX"; "Chapter Two: Trick or Treat, Freak"; "Chapter Three: The Pollywog").

Hopper is also late. Chronically, repeatedly, late. Worse, he often forgets to call. He tries to amend his temporal transgressions with candy, meals, and other symbols of deep affection for Eleven, but after a series of these exchanges, viewers sense the rising tension between him and Eleven. If Hopper's parenting style and Eleven's latchkey status ring familiar for many Gen Xers, so does the eventual boiling over of family tension. Like many parents, Hopper prioritizes safety, and, like many children, Eleven desires freedom. Even after it is okay for the community to know Eleven is alive, Hopper still limits what she can do, for example, instructing that she not go to the mall. Given Eleven's history of isolation and imprisonment at the lab, it is no wonder she finds Hopper's family cabin—cozy and "idyllic rural" as it is—a cage nonetheless. In Season Two's "Chapter Three: The Pollywog," Eleven ultimately decides to leave the cabin and is spotted by a mother pushing her daughter on a swing. In "Chapter Four: Will the Wise," Hopper and Eleven argue about this encounter:

Hopper: "You put us in danger!" [note Hopper's use of the
collective "us"—he is committed]
Eleven: "Nothing ever happens!"
Hopper: "Yeah, nothing ever happens, and you stay safe!"
[slams hand on dresser]
Eleven: "You lie!"
Hopper: "I don't lie, I protect! And I feed. And I teach. All
I ask of you is that you follow three simple rules. Three.
Rules. And ya know what? You can't even do that!"

Hopper proceeds to ground Eleven, which is somewhat comical
in its own right when one considers her powers. When he tries
to take her TV away, she prevents him from doing so. He esca-
lates the punishment—grounding her for two weeks, then three
weeks, then a month. At this point, Eleven draws a parallel:

Eleven: "You are like Papa."
Hopper: "Really? I'm like that psychotic son of a bitch?
Alright. You wanna go back in the lab? One phone call I
can make that happen." ("Chapter Four: Will the Wise")

The scene concludes as Eleven, frustrated beyond words, blows
out every window in the cabin with her power. The tension and
anger parallel the family angst present in 1980s popular culture.
After Eleven's destruction of her physical home—and perhaps
her family "home" with Hopper—she continues her search for
home-as-sanctuary by seeking out her biological family.

Bonded by Blood: Eleven, Aunt Becky, and Mama

When cleaning the cabin, Eleven discovers a space hidden in
the floor where Hopper stores boxes of sensitive documents:

material pertaining to his family, Vietnam, and the Hawkins Lab. Within these documents, Eleven finds photos of Papa and her biological mother whom she contacts with her powers ("Chapter Four: Will the Wise"). Seemingly convinced that Hopper's house is not a home, Eleven hitches a ride to meet Terry (Mama) in person. Things seem positive and supportive upon arrival, and viewers wonder if blood is the necessary requirement to feel at home. Becky, Mama's sister, tells Eleven that their home is her home and does not push for details regarding Eleven's whereabouts—just that Eleven can talk when she is ready to do so.

The audience soon learns, however, that biological relatives have faults and agendas, too. Through flickering lights and static-filled TV, Eleven realizes that Mama wants to "talk." Using her powers, Eleven flashes back with her, and we see a series of images, including Eleven's birth as well as mothers at Hawkins Lab visiting their children. We also see Aunt Becky, along with Papa, explaining to Mama that Eleven did not survive childbirth, even though she hears Eleven crying. Additionally, we see Mama entering Hawkins Lab with a pistol and shooting a guard. We also see Eleven playing with another girl, and finally, we see Mama being electro-shocked by Papa into her current vegetative state. Eleven's biological aunt, it seems, has been part of the conspiracy all along. It is at this point that Eleven catches Becky on the phone with the authorities, which ends any hope Eleven has of finding a home among her blood relatives ("Chapter Five: Dig Dug").

Eleven's brief connection with her biological family is significant for many reasons. For one, it continues *Stranger Things'* penchant for turning our taken-for-granted assumptions about family and trust upside down, as it were. Not everyone has a dependable, honorable, supportive, or ethical family to rely upon—a house to call a home. Second, the exchange sets Eleven up for the next phase of her quest for home because she finds information on the girl she was playing with at the lab, thus presenting viewers with another potential definition of home and family.

Sweet Soul "Sister": Eleven and Eight

The mystery playmate from the lab, we learn, is Kali—designation #008. If "home" was unattainable from an emotionally compromised, overprotective sheriff, and remained elusive among her biological relatives, perhaps Eleven can find a sense of home and family with a pseudo-sister who shared Eleven's trauma. Indeed, the episode's title, "The Lost Sister," not only continues *Stranger Things'* redefinition of what constitutes family but also implies some, however small, hope for connection. As with previous encounters, Eleven's interaction with Kali seems initially promising:

> Eleven: "What's wrong?"
> Kali: "Nothing is wrong. I just feel a hole—a piece of me was missing. Now it's not. Does that make sense?"
> Eleven: "Yes."
> Kali: "I think your mother sent you here for a reason. I think she somehow knew that we belong together. I think this is your home."
> Eleven: "Home."
> Kali: "Yes. Home." ("Chapter Seven: The Lost Sister")

More internal conflict awaits Eleven, however. On the one hand, she has found another group of outcasts. One, Kali, is very much like her; she has different powers, but is powered nonetheless—and thus can relate to Eleven as no one else can. Eleven looks for identifying tattoos from the lab among Kali's cohort and finds none, but Kali reminds her, "like us, they're outcasts." Eleven asks Kali what she means by outcasts, to which Kali replies: "Society left them behind. Hurt them. Discarded them" ("Chapter Seven: The Lost Sister"). This group of outcasts differs greatly from Eleven's "geeky" cohort in Hawkins. Instead of playing games and riding bikes, Kali's outcasts exact revenge upon "bad men," specifically anyone who played a role in her Hawkins Lab imprisonment:

Eleven: "You kill them?"
Kali: "They're criminals. We simply make them pay for their crimes." ("Chapter Seven: The Lost Sister")

On the other hand, despite outward appearances, Eleven is divided on many fronts. She is scarred from her experience at Hawkins Lab, but uncomfortable with Kali's vigilante justice; she is happy to have found a "sister" in Chicago, but feeling an inexorable pull toward her circle of outcasts in Hawkins. She still hears Hopper calling for her over the CB, and when Kali instructs her to embrace her anger as a means of magnifying her power, Eleven centers on Hawkins. She thinks about a jealous memory of Max talking to Mike, of her argument with Hopper, and Hopper explaining that her mom is gone. Eventually Eleven must make a choice: to violently dispense justice to those who wronged her, setting her on a violent life course, or to help protect her endangered friends in Hawkins. Kali points out that her friends in Hawkins cannot save her, but Eleven knows she can save them. On the bus back to Indiana, Eleven says she is "going home" ("Chapter Seven: The Lost Sister").

Father Figure: Eleven and Jim, Part Two

Eleven's search for "home" culminates in the Season Two finale. As Hopper and Eleven drive along, Eleven explains how she hitched a ride with a man in a big truck to see Terry. Hopper, again assuming the role of concerned parent, worries about Eleven hitching rides in big trucks with strange men. Then, he drops his guard:

> Hopper: "Sometimes I feel like I'm—like I'm just some kinda black hole or somethin.'"
> Eleven: "Black hole?"
> Hopper: "Yeah. It's a, ya know, it's this thing in outer space. It's like, it sucks everything towards it and destroys it. Sara had a picture book about outer space. She loved it."
> Eleven: "Who's Sara?"
> Hopper: "Sara? Sara's my girl. She's my little girl."
> Eleven: "Where is she?"
> Hopper: "Well, that's kinda the thing, kid. She, she left us."
> Eleven: "Gone."
> Hopper: "Yeah, in a black hole. It got her. And somehow, I've just been scared, ya know? I've just been scared it would take you, too. I think that's why I get so mad. I'm so sorry for everything. I can be so, so . . .'"
> Eleven: "Stupid."
> Hopper: "Yeah, stupid. Really stupid." ("Chapter Nine: The Gate")

The season closes with Hopper obtaining a birth certificate for "Jane Hopper" from Dr. Owens. On the one hand, Hopper's adoption of Eleven represents another triumph for the idea of nontraditional family and asks viewers to question the "normalcy" of the traditional nuclear family. On the other hand, given the amount of institutional cynicism present in *Stranger Things*, it is somewhat surprising that their relationship requires sanction in any official sense.

Father Figure: Eleven and Jim, Part Three

In Season Three, Hopper is home more, and we gain a glimpse into his life with Eleven. He appears (slightly) more comfortable with his role as Eleven's father. We learn that Hopper and Eleven have developed a routine; for example, they enjoy making triple-decker Eggo waffles for breakfast, playing board games every night, and watching old westerns on television. Despite his faults, and they are numerous, Hopper is both physically and emotionally more present. In the opening episode of the season, Hopper is trying to parent, woefully unprepared to deal with a teenage daughter, particularly one who recently started dating. He asks Joyce for assistance, hoping she can help him put some much needed space between Eleven and her boyfriend, Mike. Joyce helps Hopper write and practice a powerful speech, a speech meant to start a dialogue about respect and boundaries between him and Eleven. Ultimately, Hopper does not adhere to the speech, opting to threaten Mike instead. He warns Mike to give Eleven some space.

These scenes with Joyce are powerful for two reasons. One, Joyce is the "savior" for Hopper's family, as opposed to Hopper being the savior for hers, thus flipping the script on the Bob-as-patriarchal-savior storyline in Season Two. Despite this flip of the script, however, Hopper still tries to fulfill the role of savior to Joyce. Later in the season, Hopper is concerned Joyce might move out of Hawkins. Like his desire to provide for and protect Eleven, he wants to do the same for Joyce. He tells her,

"It is important to me that you feel safe. . . . I want you to feel like this can still be your home" ("Chapter Three: The Case of the Missing Lifeguard"). Yet, at the end of Season Three, much like Bob, it is clear Hopper cannot protect Joyce or her children. Two, the scenes also reiterate, once again, how *all* types of families struggle with interpersonal communication. While Hopper has difficulties speaking to Eleven, so do Joyce and Karen with their children.

In the end, Eleven's quest provides an opportunity to explore, challenge, and validate the myriad of understandings of home and family that many Gen Xers experienced as children. And, as the above sections demonstrate, relations between parents (broadly defined) and children are not always smooth. One thing the outcasts in the 1980s dataset and *Stranger Things* have in common is absentee parents to some degree—either literally or figuratively. As the next section outlines, this absenteeism can put undue pressure on Gen X children to save their family or "home."

Parents Just Don't Understand: Types of Parents in 1980s Pop Culture

According to Howe and Strauss, Gen Xers were born nearly equally to Silent Generation and Baby Boomer parents (*13th Gen*, 55). The Silent Generation, in particular, had a profound impact on Gen X, as many held positions of authority beyond being parents (doctors, teachers, professors, and politicians) when Gen Xers were coming of age. While Silents and Gen Xers have some aspects in common, namely a "sense of generational inadequacy and an awkward location in U.S. history," they are also vastly different (Howe and Strauss, *13th Gen*,

39). Silents are considered to be the wealthiest generation in America; on the other hand, Gen Xers faced a harsh economic reality as they entered adulthood. Little Gen Xers were also often seen as roadblocks to Silents, as Silents sought to recapture their youth (Howe and Strauss, *13th Gen*, 40). This led to strained relationships, as Silent parents "began to feel a very real disappointment in their kids—and they let their kids know it" (Howe and Strauss, *13th Gen*, 40). This disappointment manifested itself in different ways. In the next two sections, I explore two different types of parents: absent and overbearing.

Literal and Figurative Absence

Parents are problematic whether they are literally absent (absentee dads in *Stranger Things* and *E.T. the Extra-Terrestrial*), figuratively absent (dad in *Big*, Cameron's dad in *Ferris Bueller's Day Off*), or involved. Throughout these artifacts, we see parents continually let down their children by being both literally and figuratively absent. As mentioned in the previous section, in Season Two of *Stranger Things* Hopper constantly makes promises to Eleven, yet he never follows through on or lives up to them. Despite always having a reason or an excuse, the simple fact is he is busy and prioritizes his job. He attempts to mitigate his shortcomings with promises of candy and television time, but to Eleven these are not adequate substitutes. While Hopper seems to genuinely care for Eleven, it is hard to see his motives as completely genuine. While Hopper is serving as Eleven's pseudo father, Eleven is serving as Hopper's pseudo daughter, filling a deep void after the loss of his own. Additionally, in a similar fashion, we also see Karen repeatedly let down her daughter Nancy, and Max's mother let down Max. Karen isn't emotionally available to talk to Nancy about her struggles with

Steve and Jonathan, and Max's parents are absent for nearly the entire second season, as Max's brother, Billy, torments Max and bullies her new friends. They are also absent in the third season when Billy becomes possessed and terrorizes the entire town.

In other instances, parents care, but for a variety of reasons, they are oblivious to what is going on with their children. For example, in *Ferris Bueller's Day Off*, Ferris's mom is quick to baby Ferris when he reports he is not feeling well; despite this level of concern, she is shocked when she realizes Ferris has already missed nine days of school. When discussing Ferris's absences, Principal Rooney states, "That's probably because he wasn't sick. He was skipping school. Wake up and smell the coffee, Mrs. Bueller. It's a fool's paradise. He is just leading you down the primrose path" (*Ferris Buller's Day Off*). Other examples of well-intentioned, yet clueless, parents include parents in *E.T. the Extra-Terrestrial*, *Gremlins*, *The Breakfast Club*, and *Big*. In all of these movies, life-changing/altering events are happening to children within their homes, but the parents fail to realize what is occurring until the event becomes, in some instances, downright dangerous. For example, in *Gremlins* the parents fail to realize there is a growing gremlin population in their son's room. The dad is too busy with his inventions, and the mother, more often than not, is concerned with kitchen-related tasks. On the other hand, other parents within the 1980s dataset are not even well-intentioned; they are checked out and more concerned about their own affairs, like Lieutenant Thompson in *Nightmare on Elm Street* and Allison's parents in *The Breakfast Club*.

As seen in the 1980s dataset, the absence of nurturing and reliable parental figures puts undue pressure on the children to "save" the family. In *Back to the Future*, Marty is literally trying to make his dysfunctional family (detached father, vodka-soaked mother, underachieving siblings) reappear. In *The Goonies*, Mikey wonders, "What are we going to do about the country club? It is killing our parents!" This desire to save the nuclear family is another testament to the power of the nuclear family in 1980s popular culture as discussed earlier in this chapter as well as how much pressure is placed on children to save it; no matter how dysfunctional a nuclear family may be, the desire to preserve and save it is strong. The burden to save it, however, is placed not on the parents but rather the children, as is the case with Marty in *Back to the Future* and the children in *The Goonies*.

In *Nightmare on Elm Street* we see a similar motif and another mother drowning in booze. Despite her friends being murdered and not sleeping for days, Nancy ends up serving as an emotional support and caregiver for her mother. More specifically, in *Nightmare on Elm Street*, families are threatened by not only Freddy Krueger and his assault on teens, the next generation of Elm Street, but also the families themselves. In his article "Everyday Nightmares: The Rhetoric of Social Horror in the Nightmare on Elm Street Series," Gary Heba notes: "Alcoholism, neglect, abuse, and sexual molestation are all woven into the family tapestry of the *Nightmare* movies, such that most of the parents become 'monsters' along with Freddy" (113). For Gen Xers, danger can come from both outside and from within. In each of the above examples, parents expect their children to parent and provide support.

Excessive Presence

Parents, however, are also problematic when they are involved. In several instances in the artifacts analyzed, parents pressure their children to do better in different ways: in sports, in school, and within the family. For example, in *The Breakfast Club*, Andrew describes the pressure his dad places on him to be a superior athlete. Impersonating his dad, he shares with his peers, "I won't tolerate any losers in this family." Brian, when describing the B he received in shop class and the pressures he feels as home to succeed as a student, contemplates suicide. In both examples, the actions of parents caused their children to make poor choices, ultimately costing them a Saturday of detention. In the case of Brian, however, the impact of excessive presence could have been much worse. He could have died by suicide.

In *Stranger Things* we do not see parents who are excessively present, except maybe Dustin's mom in Season Two. While she may not be excessively physically present/with Dustin at all times, she does appear to be excessively *emotionally* present. She relies on Dustin for her primary companionship, and because she "needs" his companionship, she often refuses to recognize when Dustin needs help and parenting, namely when he hid Dart, a dangerous creature from the Upside Down world, in his bedroom. Naturally, children such as Dustin growing up in dysfunctional surroundings look elsewhere for support. For Gen Xers, support often came from alternative authority figures and popular culture itself.

You Spin Me Round (Like a Record): Substitutes for Parental Bonds

When the family unit is tarnished, children often are cast as heroes up against adult villains. Commonly, these villains are the people children interact with the most: parents and teachers. Jonathon I. Oake writes: "In *Ferris Bueller's Day Off*, for instance, the adolescent protagonist comes up against a variety of older authority figures (parents, schoolteachers), all of whom are met-onymically identified with the world of grown-ups. It is implicit here that youth is not understood as a primarily developmen-tal or biological concept but as a social formation that stands in resistance toward grown-up society" (85). As noted above, such resistance toward authority figures leads to unmistakable bonds between peers being formed. It is not a coincidence that one of the two taglines used for Season One of *Stranger Things* was "a friend is someone you would do anything for." In sum, to combat parental shortcomings and teachers' misdoings, Gen X children turned to "ourselves, our peers, global images and products" for guidance (Kitwana, 7). This social cohesion is evident in varying degrees within every artifact of this study's dataset. In addition to their relationships with peers, as they forged through adolescence, Gen Xers found other parental surrogates: teachers with "child-like" spirits as well as popular culture of the time—video games, movies, and television. In the next section, I introduce these surrogate relationships.

Teachers

Throughout 1980s popular culture, we see archetypal *good* teachers, readily available to help their students and mitigate the shortcomings of their students' parents (Doc in *Back to the Future I* and *II*, Mr. Keating in *Dead Poets Society*, and Mr. Hanson in *Gremlins*). Despite this recurring representation, the American educational system as a whole is often portrayed as bleak and unbending, reflecting what was eerily echoed in Pink Floyd's 1979 hit "Another Brick in The Wall (Part 2)": "we don't need no education / we don't need no thought con-trol." Even when coming-of-age Gen Xers are able to find a positive aspect to their education, such as a favorite teacher, the overwhelming weight of the crumbling institution is often felt. Generally speaking, Gen Xers were leery of educational institutions, and this perspective was reflected in and shaped popular culture. When they are able to find a teacher to connect with, the teacher also is susceptible to the shortcomings of the institution, sometimes paying with his/her career and life.

For example, within the 1980s dataset, there are a) representations of bumbling administrators who fail miserably at connecting with students (Mr. Rooney in *Ferris Bueller's Day Off*), b) cynical administrators who despise the very population they are supposed to mentor (Mr. Vernon in *The Breakfast Club* and Mr. Strickland in *Back to the Future*), and c) teachers who are unable to embrace alternative perspectives and see beyond the educational institution itself (most teachers in *Dead Poets Society*). As the teenagers in *The Breakfast Club* write in their essay to Mr. Vernon, "You see us as you want to see us—in the simplest terms, in the most convenient definitions. But what we found out is that each one of us is a brain . . . and an athlete . . . and a basket case . . . a princess . . . and a criminal" (*The Breakfast Club*). These teenagers, much like Gen Xers in the 1980s, recognize that the institution that is supposed to foster their intellectual and emotional development is riddled with cynical professionals, held by powerful institutional bindings and biases.

Many of these professionals, like Mr. Vernon, draw heavily on stereotypes, characterizing all students as lazy. In extreme cases, the professionals actively despise the children they are supposed to protect and educate. For example, Mr. Rooney becomes obsessed with punishing the truant Ferris, mumbling at one point, "I'm going to catch this kid and put one helluva dent in his future. Fifteen years from now when he looks back on the ruin that he's become, he is going to remember Edward Rooney" (*Ferris Buller's Day Off*). In another example, in *Stand by Me*, Chris is framed by his teacher, who took the money Chris stole and then, after feeling guilty, gave back. She uses it to buy herself a new outfit, knowing full well others would continue to blame Chris for the missing cash. This is devastating for Chris, seeing firsthand how someone who is supposed to believe in him, to protect him, did not.

In *Stranger Things* school is both a sanctuary and a site of struggle, depending on what point one is at in the series. As Ludovic A. Sourdot, associate professor of education, writes: "In the last chapter of Season One, Hawkins Middle School goes from being a resource and a place of comfort to becoming a site of struggle between Eleven and the federal agents. In the end, schools and schooling are depicted as a site of suffering (bullying), comfort (the assembly in Will's honor), resource (thanks to its dedicated educators), struggle (where good defeats evil) and hope (the school dance)" (212). Throughout it all, however, the children have a positive bond with one of their teachers, Mr. Clarke. He serves as a reminder there is good even within a decaying institution.

Perhaps the greatest contrast between "good" teachers and the grinding institutional underlings is in *Dead Poets Society*. In this movie, there is a stark contrast between Mr. Keating and the rest of the faculty. The science, Latin, and trigonometry teachers are very traditional—and mirror the traditional "nuclear" family structure seen within this movie and others. In one scene, the trigonometry instructor urges his students "not to test" him on his homework policy, echoing Neil's dad, who is unbending in regard to Neil's education. For these instructors, and many parents in 1980s popular culture, adolescence is about obedience and rigor. In contrast, Mr. Keating, a newly hired English teacher, strolls into his classroom whistling. In his first lesson, he asks students to walk out of the classroom with him into the entryway. It is here he delivers one of the most famous lines of the 1980s, "O Captain, My Captain" (*Dead Poets Society*). Throughout the movie Keating strives to identify with his students, not subdue or break them. This is very different from many educators represented in 1980s popular culture. In 1980s popular culture, the "good" teachers are often punished for their work. Keating is ultimately fired in *Dead Poets Society*, Mr. Hanson in *Gremlins* dies, and future Doc is committed to a mental institution in *Back to the Future II*.

Like the movies in the dataset, the children in *Stranger Things* have a special bond with a teacher: Mr. Clarke, who represents "the only constant meaningful presence in [Hawkins] education community," and as a reminder that father figures in *Stranger Things* are absent for these characters (Sourdot, 212). Their relationship parallels the relationship of Billy and his science teacher Mr. Hanson in *Gremlins*. In both, teachers—not parents—help the children who are curious or struggling. However, unlike *Gremlins* and other movies in the dataset, in *Stranger Things*, Mr. Clarke has a positive relationship with the boys *and* keeps his job and his life. In Seasons One and Two, he is often the first person the boys go to when they need help, and he appears to always try to give the best advice. In Season Three, he also helps Joyce learn more about electromagnetic fields. Unlike teachers within the 1980s dataset, nothing detrimental comes of his relationship with the children or Joyce. Like single parentage, this is another way in which *Stranger Things* challenges the representations within the dataset. It is possible to have positive influences, and these positive influences will prevail, even within problematic institutions.

Popular Culture

In many movies in the 1980s dataset, another substitute for parental bond, or light in the absence of, is popular culture. In some ways, households plagued by divorce, or parents busy "finding themselves," solidified Gen X's deep connection with, and affection for, popular culture, as television became a "baby-sitter, teacher, friend, and entertainer" (Owen, 42). The impact popular culture had on Xers was profound, as "television imprinted this generation—starting with the children's TV show 'Sesame Street' and then on to darker cable fare" (O'Donovan, 17). For example, in *E.T. the Extra-Terrestrial* the opening shot shows children occupied with Dungeons & Dragons, and later in the movie, E.T. is left home alone and the only "parent" present to halt his destructive behavior is the television. Additionally, in *Ferris Bueller's Day Off* the teenagers use popular culture as a surrogate parent as they play hooky from school, traipsing around Chicago.

In his article "Portrait of the Xer as a White-Bred Suburbanite: *Mad Men* as a Generation X Understanding of the 1960s," Tom Pace discusses intra-generational (nostalgic) popular culture. He wanted to experience the sixties, his fascination piqued by the discovery of old *Life* and *Look* magazines in his grandparents' attic. From there he got into classic rock of that era—the Beatles, the Rolling Stones. Upon entering college he "finally discovered that there existed other musical genres that, as I would soon come to understand, spoke to and about Generation X—not Top 40, not classic rock, but rather rap, hip-hop, and alternative rock," including the Pixies, U2, the Replacements, Pavement, and culminating in the 1991 release of Nirvana's *Nevermind* (Pace, "Portrait of the Xer," 154). In *Stranger Things* music plays a similar role for Will, and one instance serves as a light when the parental bonds darken. The Clash's "Should I Stay or Should I Go" is not only a symbol of brotherly bonding while the parental bond disintegrates, but also an anchor for Will. It is what he quietly sings while in the alternate reality; it is what he holds on to in the dark Upside Down world.

Pace also discusses the ways in which popular culture united the "fractured, disparate group" that is Gen X ("Portrait of the Xer," 156–57). We see clear nods to this in *Stranger Things*, as the geeky protagonists bond over all manner of popular culture: Dungeons & Dragons, *Star Trek, Star Wars*, and their (mostly unified, save for two Egons) *Ghostbusters* Halloween costumes. Prominent *physical* bonding spaces utilized by *Stranger Things* are the arcade in Season Two and the mall in Season Three, which I discuss more in chapter 3.

Like many artifacts of popular culture, reviews of arcades are mixed. For example, a 1982 piece in the *Christian Science Monitor* points out that "vidkids" skip school to play video games and that parents tend to blame the games (rather than themselves) for behavioral problems (Scott). However, psychologist Mike Wessels argues that "these games provide a tremendous medium to build mastery and self-confidence" (quoted in Duke). Of course, self-confidence can be fleeting when a new kid takes the high score in Dig Dug. Kyle Riismandel argues that the arcade served multiple functions in the late 1970s and early 1980s. First, the arcade was seen as a safe place for parents to drop off their children—surely a luxury given the domestic and professional changes occurring in American families at the time. Additionally, as the arcade industry matured, so did the surveillance and safety techniques developed to mitigate bad behavior. Second, Riismandel argues, the arcade (and by extension the suburban malls that housed

many arcades) became home for teenagers, or, as one inter-
viewee from a 1983 *Washington Post* article puts it, the arcade
is "more home than home" (quoted in Riismandel, 66). A teen
interviewed for an earlier *Washington Post* piece said the arcade
represents "a community of friends" (quoted in Riismandel,
68). The arcade is a place friendly to outcasts, like the *Stranger
Things* kids, as evidenced by Riismandel's review of counter-
culture arcade kids who feel they have no home (figuratively
or literally) outside the arcade.

Sweet Home Suburbia: The Rise of
Interpersonal and Financial Problems

In this chapter, I explore how *Stranger Things* parallels 1980s
representations of family in popular culture, specifically the
decay of the traditional nuclear family, the evolving and revolv-
ing definition of home, and the varying types of problematic
parent-child relationships. While there are a vast number of
similarities between the 1980s dataset and the series, one way
in which the dataset and *Stranger Things* are different is that,
unlike the movies in the dataset, *Stranger Things* champions,
but does not valorize, single parentage via the Byers family,
suggesting that the best home for children may not always be
the home with two parents. Throughout *Stranger Things* we see
that single parents, and sometimes even friendships with peers
and trusted authority figures, can offer the best support systems
for adolescents. The boys are able to save their friend because
of their strong bond and friendship, ultimately with the help
of other outcasts: a single parent, an emotionally fragile sheriff,
and a trusted science teacher.

The stark contrast between the Byers family and the Wheeler family demonstrates that in certain circumstances, it is better for children if their parents divorce. It also demonstrates that the sprawl of suburbia does not guarantee safety, happiness, or a home. While a commonly cited reason for moving to the suburbs was the "safety" the big city cannot provide (most notably in *Big*), *Stranger Things* suggest this is not the case. (In *Big*, when Josh arrives in the city, he is confronted with prostitutes and homeless individuals; he hears gunshots, as he tries to sleep in his rundown motel room. This is quite different from his hometown, where he rode his bike, alone, in the street.) Despite these contrasts, however, all families within the dataset struggle to some degree and are burdened not only with interpersonal problems but also financial ones. This ultimately contributes to and reflects Gen X's growing institutional cynicism. In the next chapter, I review the economic landscape of the 1980s, discussing the widening income gap and the growing emphasis on materialism. This gap, and the rise of conspicuous consumption, is reflected in 1980s popular culture and in *Stranger Things*, reflecting and reinforcing Gen X's cynical appraisal of troubled times.

— 3 —
Opportunity (Let's Make Lots of Money)
1980s American Economy

Economic reviews from the 1980s were mixed. David S. Myers's study of major newspaper editorials indicated that "economic concerns were the most influential" during the 1980 presidential campaign (414). Other period pieces debate whether or not the US economy was in decline or renewal (Huntington) or note regionally unequal trends of economic expansion and contraction (Jackson and Masnick). Political scientists John E. Schwarz and Thomas Volgy take a different approach in their analysis. Arguing that Reagan's policies of reduced regulation and tax cuts (and the policies of his like-minded political allies) were based on a faulty assumption that the American economy was in decline, they claim that the economy of the 1970s performed well across the board, but (1) the price of oil and (2) a surge in the labor force (i.e., overall number of workers) gave the *appearance* of a sluggish economy and thus the need for government intervention. Ironically, federal intervention contributed to the very uncertainty said interventions were designed to alleviate, and "both added to the number of impoverished Americans and widened the income gap between wealthy and poor Americans" (Schwarz and Volgy, 99).

For some, the widening income gap and the emphasis on materialism marked a new-yet-old redefinition of the American Dream. For example, Lawrence Samuel notes that the American Dream always included some sense of being one's own boss, and the idea that, through hard work, individuals from across the social spectrum could attain a better, more fulfilling life (13). The egalitarian nature of the Dream waned in the 1920s as the "wild pursuit of money and the things it could buy" resulted in fulfillment for only a few (Samuel, 13). Some sense of egalitarianism and collectivism returned to the Dream during and following the Great Depression, but soon after World War II, emergent neoliberal rhetoric warned that big government and high taxes would destroy the American Dream as citizens looked to the government for "handouts" (Samuel, 44). Thus, with the election of a deregulation-minded Reagan, the American Dream's pendulum swung back toward the individualistic and materialistic.

More recent social commentary questioned if the American Dream had in fact become the American Myth. While economists debated whether the economy was growing or not, the widening income gap was all but ignored. According to Linda Tirado, author of *Hand to Mouth: Living in Bootstrap America*: "When you think about it the minimum wage peaked in 1968, and through the early '70s you could still, on minimum wage, pay for a university degree, so this kind of flattening out of the American Dream and this inaccessibility of that basic contract of 'work hard, be able to live a reasonable life' has been fairly recent" ("Flyover"). Those expecting a middle-class existence in the 1980s were disillusioned as job insecurity increased, wages decreased, and income inequality—even among those of similar experience and achievement—grew wider (Carnevale). During this time, all men under twenty-five saw a 15 percent earnings drop, and non–college degree men in their late twenties saw a 10 percent earnings drop (Howe and Strauss, *13th Gen*, 94). While women fared slightly better, they also experienced a decrease in wages. More so than any other generation, Gen X bore the consequences of the country's increased economic uncertainty.

In addition to decreased wages, Gen Xers also watched as age-based entitlements, once set aside for youth, were redistributed to the elderly. For the first time in history, children (Gen Xers) became the most poverty-prone population (Howe and Strauss, *13th Gen*, 36). These factors increased Gen X's distrust in the American economy, and the role the government played in it. In their early adulthood, Gen X's distrust led to apathy toward politics, and this increased apathy led Gen X to place "little importance on citizenship and national identity" relative to their predecessors (Halstead). This perspective marshaled a deep incredulity that permeated popular culture.

In this chapter, I explore not only how Gen X's economic cynicism influenced movies of the 1980s but also how, in turn, these movies reinforced and validated the cynicism of Gen Xers who watched these movies on the small and large screen. I start by exploring how the widening income gap is portrayed in the 1980s dataset and *Stranger Things*. Within the 1980s dataset, most of the movies showcase the widening income gap and reinforce that a middle-class lifestyle is much easier to live than a lower-class one. Unlike movies in previous decades (for example, *Rocky* and *Funny Girl*), many of the movies in the 1980s, and all the movies within the 1980s dataset, challenge, at least in part, the new-yet-old American Dream, a narrative that purports the belief that "we can all succeed if we work hard, even (perhaps especially) those who begin in poverty or other difficult circumstances" (Kidd, 81).

It is within the 1980s dataset that the American Myth is explored. Although the 1980s dataset challenges the American Dream narrative by including characters from different socio-economic classes and showing how each lives, the movies within the dataset ultimately fail to explore the relationship between economic power and social and political power. This greatly limits the scope of any critique of the American Dream and American Myth, as viewers are left with mostly surface-level observations in regard to the economy.

Additionally, many of the movies within the 1980s dataset reinforce the idea that money and consumption bring happiness and prestige. Throughout this chapter I explore the proliferation of materialism in the 1980s, namely how conspicuous consumption created an economic paradox for Gen Xers. Struggling to make ends meet, many Gen Xers spent money they did not have in order to acquire or maintain prestige associated with material goods and corresponding socioeconomic status. I also examine how, within the 1980s dataset, depictions of conspicuous consumption in popular culture often were linked in popular culture to waning community health and cultural loss. I argue that the unprecedented growth of media conglomerates in the 1980s, many of which produced the films within the 1980s dataset, serves as a microcosm for what was happening in America. As conglomerates multiplied and flourished, alternative viewpoints were inherently limited. Jeff Gordinier, Gen X author and journalist, notes how these massive media companies were "set up to maximize profits, not to worry about art" (13). Much in the same fashion, as income and social inequality worsened in the United States, fewer and fewer people had a voice.

Regardless of Gen X's own consumption (and that consumption was profound), cultural loss is a point of great concern for Gen Xers, and this concern appears in popular culture of the time period. Of note, this was of particular concern to Xers as they watched the rise of millennial music in the late 1990s. Referring to this music, Gordinier writes, "The status quo was baked right into the music. If Gen-X music tended to sound as though it came from a specific place—Seattle or Manchester, Compton or Minneapolis of the South Bronx—the new millennial soundtrack came across as geographically blank" (72). Gen Xers, who hated the idea of art being influenced and controlled by corporate interests, reeled at the decade- and grunge-ending arrival of Britney Spears and other former Mickey Mouse Club Mousketeers such as Christina Aguilera and Justin Timberlake.

Finally, I examine Gen X's attitude toward the economy and how this attitude is represented within the 1980s dataset and *Stranger Things*, paying particular attention to the voices of Gen Xers who were hit hard by a shaky economy. Throughout both the 1980s dataset and series, we see how Gen X is individualistic yet sympathetic to the plights of individuals. For those in the 1980s dataset struggling to overcome the widening income gap, we see a "taking back what is mine" attitude, an attitude that has both cultivated institutional cynicism and reinforced the capitalistic underpinnings of the American Dream. Despite being hurt financially by Reagan administration policies, many Gen Xers embraced the self-reliant spirit behind said policies, notwithstanding their own cynical appraisals of the American Dream. We begin, however, with how the widening gap is portrayed in popular culture, namely how it reflects and influences Gen X's perspective toward the American economy.

Glory Days? The Widening Income Gap
and the American Myth

In the 1980s dataset, Gen X's rising cynicism due to the widening income gap is by far the most noticeable in *The Goonies*,
in which an entire residential neighborhood is threatened by
economic development. The developers want the land to build
a country club, an exclusive landmark often used to symbol-
ize and celebrate 1980s wealth. As noted by the magazine *The
Economist*, country clubs are traditionally places "where affluent, white (mostly Protestant) Americans could get together
to play golf, drink, eat mediocre food, and casually discuss
business" ("The Country-Club Vote"). A good number of
Americans were excluded from this environment because
of the cost of membership dues, further limiting their economic opportunities, as clubs were often the site of business
deals. The country club is featured in other 1980s movies and
1980s-inspired television series (*Caddyshack*, *Caddyshack II*,
and *Red Oaks*), and the plots to them are similar, focusing
on the tension between the haves (those who are welcomed
as country club members) and the have-nots (those who are
not welcomed as members, work at the country club, or are
displaced by one). The country club haves, in most instances,
found success in the expanding stock market and the economic
policies put forth by the Reagan administration, policies often
examined in popular culture.

In *Ferris Bueller's Day Off*, the economics teacher lectures
to his disinterested high school class (students yawn/sleep,
chew gum, and stare blankly across the room) about "voodoo"
economics, a term coined by Reagan's opponents to refer to
"supply-side policies that claimed tax cuts for the rich would
unleash so much growth that they'd generate enough revenue to

fund themselves" (Rampell). Because of how Reagan's administration favored this type of economic policy, voodoo economics
would later be known as Reaganomics. Ultimately, the belief
that tax cuts for businesses would result in increased spending
did not turn out as planned. Trying to explain this to his students, the economics teacher drones:

> In 1930, the Republican-controlled House of Representatives,
> in an effort to alleviate the effects of the ... Anyone? Anyone?
> ... the Great Depression, passed the ... Anyone? Anyone?
> The tariff bill? The Hawley-Smoot Tariff Act? Which, any-
> one? Raised or lowered? ... raised tariffs, in an effort to
> collect more revenue for the federal government. Did it work?
> Anyone? Anyone know the effects? It did not work, and the
> United States sank deeper into the Great Depression. Today
> we have a similar debate over this. Anyone know what this is?
> Class? Anyone? Anyone? Anyone seen this before? The Laffer
> Curve. Anyone know what this says? It says that at this point
> on the revenue curve, you will get exactly the same amount
> of revenue as at this point. This is very controversial. Does
> anyone know what Vice President Bush called this in 1980?
> Anyone? Something-d-o-o economics. "Voodoo" economics.
> (*Ferris Bueller's Day Off*)

This scene is yet another example of an institutional pillar, in
this case a teacher, unable to connect with Gen X students; as
noted previously, this is a common motif within the 1980s
dataset. Additionally, the scene also highlights how many Gen
Xers were not only disinterested and dismissive of institutional
underlings, but also of knowing the intricacies of the policies
(in this case economic) implemented by the underlings on
behalf of a larger institutional force.

The Evil Developer Movie

For the most part, only the wealthy and business owners benefit from these policies, people like the economic developers in *The Goonies*. In *The Goonies* it is made clear to viewers that one of the men attempting to buy the neighborhood did well in the expanding stock market. He is a stark contrast to the kids and families being forced out of their homes who did not reap any of the same benefits from the market or Reagan's voodoo economics. Throughout the movie, the primary means to demonstrate different economic classes is aesthetics. There is a definite aesthetic contrast between the haves and the have-nots, the greatest contrast being between the families on the verge of being displaced and the developers. Even though this particular trope has been around for years in cinema (e.g., *You Can't Take It With You* and *It's a Wonderful Life*), the 1980s gave rise to the "evil developer" movie. Within this emerging and proliferating microgenre, *The Goonies* is arguably the centerpiece.

As noted above, the 1980s was "a time of real-life economic swings, from the high inflation and interest rates of the early 1980s—followed by a recession—to the Savings and Loan Crisis of the last part of the decade" (Hogan). As many Americans struggled to pay bills, they fought foreclosures, and banks and developers became their adversaries. Because of these struggles, evil developer movies gained popularity with audiences, as many Americans wanted to see people like themselves fight (and ultimately win) against those responsible for their pain. During this time period, because of their popularity, the number of movies within this microgenre proliferated, going well beyond the dataset: *Summer Rental*, *One Crazy Summer*, and *Batteries Not Included*, to name a few (Hogan). Within the 1980s dataset, while we see this trope most overtly in *The*

Goonies, we also see it briefly touched upon in *Back to the Future*. In the opening sequence of the movie, we learn that Doc was forced to sell his family estate to developers, after many failed inventions. The 435 acres, which had been in his family for years, was sold to developers to build the Hill Valley Mall. This suggests that a) the American Dream is not all that easy to achieve, even for those who are incredibly intelligent, and b) developers often have the upper hand. Finally, we also see this trope in *Gremlins*.

In *Gremlins* many of the townspeople fear repossession, foreclosure, and denied services, a real concern for a good number of Americans in the early 1980s. To illustrate, when Mrs. Harris asks for an extension on her house payment, Mrs. Deagle, the bank representative, coldheartedly responds, "Mrs. Harris, the bank and I have the same purpose in life—to make money. Not to support a lot of … deadbeats!" (*Gremlins*). This is a common representation within this microgenre. Like Mrs. Deagle, characters affiliated with banks, developers, and the stock market are depicted as particularly cruel and lacking in any sort of empathy for those hurt by the recession. These characters believe that people who struggle to make ends meet, like Mrs. Harris, are deadbeats; they do not see them as victims of a tumultuous and unstable economy. Mrs. Deagle's perspective echoes the narrative subconsciously proliferated by the 1980s version of the American Dream, a narrative that is frequently questioned in 1980s film. The narrative is as follows: if people worked harder, they would be more successful, and, in turn, they would have more money. Unfortunately, this narrative promoted a very simplistic view of the country's economic system and its health as well as the opportunities available to most Americans. Many movies, like *The Goonies* and *Gremlins*, sought to challenge it.

In 1980s popular culture, some developers are more cruel than others. For example, Mrs. Deagle is characterized as particularly villainous; at one point, she even threatens to euthanize the dog of one of her employees simply because she finds the dog irritating. This vile representation was popular with audiences, including Gen Xers who flocked to theaters, because as Mark Hogan notes, "In Hollywood, the developer is never the hero." In movies, the common working American, mirroring those purchasing movie tickets across the country, is typically the hero. As is often the case in any movie, audiences yearn to see the hero outwit the villain; in this instance, the villain is the developer or bank standing in the way of the hero leading a fulfilling life and achieving the American Dream.

In *The Goonies*, the underdogs ultimately defeat the developers, but their victory does not come without an immense and well-documented struggle; throughout the movie, we see the children fight mob bosses, pirate ghosts, and the "haves" of Astoria. From the start, it is clear that the children whose families are on the verge of losing their homes have a difficult life. In many ways, this journey is simply one more roadblock among a series of them. These roadblocks come from a variety of places. Throughout the movie, their families are juxtaposed not only with the developers but also with *other local families* who are members of the current Astoria Country Club. This suggests tension not only from outside the community (the eager developers) but also from within. There is no safe space—not even in suburbia. For instance, in one scene, we see Brand, on his little pink ("borrowed") bike with training wheels, harassed by Troy, who wears an Astoria C.C. (Country Club) visor and drives a new 5.0 Mustang convertible. In the scene, Troy literally drives Brand into a ditch—just like the country club-building haves plan to do to his have-nots neighborhood.

Why Can't We Be Friends?

There are many parallels between *Stranger Things* and *The Goonies*, especially the plot itself (broadly defined): children on a shared adventure to save their community. There are also parallels between how the economy and socioeconomic class are represented. One year before Season One of *Stranger Things* is set (1982), many Americans were not pleased with the state of the economy. According to a poll at the time, 54 percent of Americans said that Reagan's policies "had made their personal financial situation worse" (Auxier). Throughout chapter 2, I discuss some of the ways in which this economic uncertainty, namely those associated with single parenthood, are represented in the series, echoing some of the same themes seen in *The Goonies*. For instance, as I note in chapter 2, *Stranger Things* makes a stark aesthetic comparison by contrasting the possessions of Mike's family (the haves) and Will's family (the have-nots), similar to the contrast depicted between Brand and Troy in *The Goonies*. While the Wheeler family/Byers family contrast serves as a way for *Stranger Things* to critique the "outward perfection" of the nuclear family, it also serves as a way to showcase the widening income gap and economic disparities in 1980s small town America. This contrast is similar to the contrast between Josh's city (adult) life and suburban (child) life in *Big*. As an adult in New York City, after securing employment, he has his own spacious loft apartment. In the suburbs, as a child, Josh must share a room with his baby sister, suggesting that money is tight in his four-person family.

Throughout *Stranger Things*, several scenes demonstrate how there are limited opportunities for upward mobility for the residents of Hawkins. In Season One, while cynically critiquing her own nuclear family, Nancy highlights how starting a life together was "easy" for her parents, noting how this is no longer the case for coming-of-age Gen Xers. She mentions how her dad had "a cushy job, money" when he married her mother ("Chapter Five: The Flea and the Acrobat"). She is not the only one to notice this change and the lack of upward mobility available to Gen Xers. In Season Two, when discussing their futures, the following exchange occurs between Steve and Nancy:

> Steve: ". . . I mean, I'm just going to end up working for my dad anyway."
> Nancy: "That's not true."
> Steve: "I dunno, Nance, is that such a bad thing? It has insurance and benefits and all that adult stuff. And if I took it, ya know, I could, could be around for our senior year." ("Chapter One: MADMAX")

The conversation between Nancy and Steve highlights the limitations and the grapple for economic advancement for Steve, who struggles to write his college entrance essay. During the 1980s, Gen Xers were faced with a future that all but required a college education even though a college education did not necessarily equate to financial success. Furthermore, this scene also depicts the pressure to secure employment upon high school graduation, a pressure felt by a good number of Gen Xers, particularly those with limited opportunities for mobility. Despite Nancy's cynicism, however, the scene highlights how different Nancy's world view is from Steve's. Because she is confident in her ability to get into college and knows her family is able to financially support her regardless, she is far less concerned.

It is worth noting, however, that Steve's concern has more to do with his intellectual ability and/or work ethic than his socioeconomic class, as he, like Nancy, is from a middle-class family. Even though Steve believes his opportunities for post-secondary schooling are limited, he ultimately knows he will be able to work at his father's store. Interestingly, in Season Three viewers find Steve not at the family furniture store, but wearing a sailor uniform and scooping ice cream at Scoops Ahoy, an ice cream parlor in the mall. We learn that Steve was unable to get into the local technical college, and as he tells his coworker Robin, his dad is "punishing" him for his series of academic missteps, not allowing him to work at the family furniture store until he improves his work ethic ("Chapter One: Suzie, Do You Copy?"). Despite this setback, viewers get the impression that Steve will eventually take over the family business, once he has additional work experience and improves his work ethic. Ultimately, Steve has a family that *can* financially support him, if needed. Not everyone in *Stranger Things* has this luxury. Other characters, such as Jonathan, do not have such a comfortable cushion.

Throughout the series, much like the differences between Joyce and Karen I discuss in chapter 2, we see stark differences between Steve and Jonathan. Their socioeconomic classes are only one way in which they are different, despite class being a motivating factor for much of their behavior. For example, Jonathan enjoys photography and music, but his hobbies are often put on hold to help support his family both financially and emotionally. On the other hand, Steve is an athlete who, at least in the first two seasons, does not work. In high school, unlike Jonathan, Steve was able to focus on his own interests (football, girls, and cars, in no particular order), as he was not forced to take on additional adult responsibilities. Like Brand and the country club teenagers in *The Goonies*, there is palpable tension between Jonathan and Steve, but the tension feels like it has less to do with class and more to do with other identity markers. Generally speaking, class is mostly a nonfactor for children and teenagers in the series.

This is one way in which the series diverges from the 1980s dataset, specifically how those in different socioeconomic classes interact with one another. In many instances, friendships blossom. This is particularly noticeable in Jonathan and Nancy's case, as their relationship develops throughout the three seasons into a romantic one. While their different socioeconomic classes do not prevent them from being romantically involved, that does not mean socioeconomic class is a nonfactor in their relationship, as there is some miscommunication and frustration between them because of it. In Season Three, for example, after they are fired from their internships at the local newspaper, Jonathan is clearly frustrated. He knows he needs the internship for both the income and networking opportunities. Nancy is much more flippant, however, reassuring him it was only a summer job. Jonathan proclaims, exasperated, "I don't live in a two-story house on Maple Street. My dad doesn't earn six figures. Hell, he isn't even around" ("Chapter Four: The Sauna Test"). Despite this argument, they persevere and their relationship continues, suggesting that friendship can transcend socioeconomic class—a relatively uncommon theme in the 1980s dataset (except maybe *The Breakfast Club*, although we get the feeling that the students went their separate ways after detention was over).

Additionally, unlike Brand and Troy (*The Goonies*), Mike and Will are friends. Brand and Troy are antagonistic toward one another with their different socioeconomic classes at the nucleus, whereas Mike and Will find common ground. This supports current research that inter-socioeconomic friendships can form, particularly in the case of children and teenagers who interact at extracurricular activities such as art and athletics (Malacarne). For Jonathan and Nancy, they came together to save their brother and friend, respectively. For the children, they bonded as members of the Hawkins Middle School AV Club. Interestingly, while the children's different socioeconomic classes are obvious to viewers, particularly in the way of material possessions seen in each of the boys' houses and in their bedrooms, the interactions between the boys suggest they are not aware, or at least they do not care, they are from different socioeconomic backgrounds. Because they are a little older, however, Jonathan and Nancy are much more aware of differences in their upbringing due to socioeconomic class.

The variance between *Stranger Things* and 1980s popular culture is reflective of more current times. Despite having set their show in the 1980s, the creators of *Stranger Things* have benefited from modern-day thought, avoiding "egregious racial and sexual stereotyping" (Smokler). Additionally, it has been well documented that the Duffer brothers listen carefully to critical and fan reception, changing entire plot lines and characters based on feedback. Ani Bundel, writer for *NBC News*, has described the Duffer brothers' approach to Season Two. She writes, "Season two was rewritten (almost wholesale) after fan and critical reaction made the show creators, the Duffer Brothers, rethink entire plotlines, recalculating the system to produce maximum enjoyment" (Bundel). While avoiding some stereotypes, such as socioeconomic class stereotypes, the Duffers still use others.

For example, it should be noted that Jonathan, who has traits that are traditionally considered feminine, is othered by many of his peers in Season One. Although he is seemingly not othered because of his socioeconomic class, he is othered for straying from hypermasculine norms, a common theme in

1980s popular culture. On the other hand, Steve, who has more masculine traits, is generally liked by most of his peers. These are problematic representations, as they reinforce gender role stereotypes and a hypermasculine, binary culture. Additionally, as noted previously, Barb, a queer character who goes missing, is nearly voiceless the entire series, while Steve is given ample opportunity and room to express himself. I discuss gender role stereotypes and racial stereotypes in chapter 5.

Despite succumbing to some stereotyping, in other ways the Duffer brothers succeed in challenging stereotypes, particularly in regard to socioeconomic class. As I note in chapter 2, one of the primary ways socioeconomic stereotypes are challenged is via the representation of family, namely how single mother Joyce demonstrates, despite hardships, that she is the most caring and competent parent in the series. In 2018, the Pew Research Center found that while approximately one fourth of solo parents and their families were living below the poverty line, current thinking around solo parenting had shifted, namely views against it had softened (Livingston). According to Gretchen Livingston, senior researcher for the Pew Research Center, "In 2012, 48% of adults agreed or strongly agreed that single parents could raise children as well as two parents can. . . . This marked a slight increase from 1994, when just 35% said as much." This softening is clearly reflected in *Stranger Things*. A good number of Gen Xers, many who were raised in single-parent households, are well-adjusted—proving a single-parent household is not an automatic sentence into delinquency. This more current perspective on single parenting is reflected in *Stranger Things*. The next section explores another aspect of the 1980s economic ecosystem—conspicuous consumption—and how this type of consumption affected all families and is portrayed in the texts is analyzed.

Material Girl: Conspicuous Consumption in the 1980s

Even though *Stranger Things* does not focus extensively on the material possessions of each of the boys, there are observable differences in both the amount and type of possessions each has. In the height of 1980s materialism, possessions were markers of wealth, an unavoidable visual representation of the widening income gap. As noted by Howe and Strauss, Gen Xers "absorbed the modern cultural message that their worth is not intrinsic, that they are only worth what others can see" (*13th Gen*, 82). For many coming-of-age Gen Xers, the more physical possessions they had, the better they felt about themselves. Gen Xers also learned that money was reliable, unlike people (Howe and Strauss, *13th Gen*, 114). Howe and Strauss note: "Having grown up in a childhood world that stressed private rights and liberties, they learned that families may leave you, neighbors may rob you, government may cheat you—but money is always faithful" (*13th Gen*, 114–15).

During the 1980s, there was a notable rise in what sociologist Thorstein Veblen calls conspicuous consumption, a type of consumption associated with acquiring luxury goods to display economic and social power. Despite what one might assume, even Gen Xers who identified as "edge-dwelling slackers" participated in conspicuous consumption (Gordinier, 103). So-called slackers "might be discreet enough to make their conspicuous consumption appear sort of casual and offhand—and therefore inconspicuous—but that doesn't mean they're consuming any less of the sumptuous enticements they used to spurn" (Gordinier, 103). It seemed as though no one in the United States was immune to this widespread contagion.

As teenagers, particularly those from middle-class and upper-class families, Gen Xers obtained a certain level of affluence due to parental subsidies (e.g., allowances) or part-time jobs. Allowances and jobs—for those who were not expected to contribute to the household income—gave Gen Xers the money to literally buy into the belief that possessions were personal markers of success. Because of this, the time period was "an exciting and euphoric spree with unfortunate long-term consequences" (Andersen). In the early 1990s, despite their economic struggles, many adult Gen Xers continued this behavior, buying material goods and flaunting the little they had to demonstrate their worth and individual competence (Howe and Strauss, *13th Gen*, 104). This led to mounting debt, and at times Gen Xers struggled to secure the most basic of necessities. The next section explores the rise of this type of consumption, the consequences that occurred as a result, and how each is explored in the 1980s dataset and *Stranger Things*.

The Rise of Conspicuous Consumption

We see consumption throughout the 1980s dataset: *Ferris Bueller's Day Off*, *The Breakfast Club*, and *Big*. In *Big*, when twelve-year-old main character Josh finds himself in an adult's body, he very quickly finds employment as an executive at a toy company. After earning his first paycheck, what follows is every child's dream—a toy store shopping spree. While Josh is not motivated by prestige or status, as he is still a child at heart, he is very much motivated by "stuff" nonetheless. Josh, however, quickly learns that the spacious New York loft apartment he rented and the numerous big ticket toys he purchased are no replacement for his parents and, ultimately, his childhood innocence. He misses his friends, and he misses his family. In the end, Josh gives up adulthood, and the pressures and pleasures that come with it, to go back to being young. Undoubtedly, this is a heartwarming message, counteracting the message prevalent in 1980s society to participate in conspicuous consumption. Not all films within the 1980s dataset, however, have similar messages. More often than not, the "power of love" was often overshadowed by the desire to earn and spend more money.

Living in Excess

Throughout the dataset, we see a contrast between those who buy and live in excess and those who can't afford to or choose (like Josh) not to live in excess: mansions versus modest housing (*Gremlins*), sushi versus cereal (*The Breakfast Club*), and functional cars versus flashy ones (*Ferris Bueller's Day Off*). One of the greatest contrasts of socioeconomic status and the ability to partake in conspicuous consumption is between Ferris and his high school principal, Edward Rooney. Film critic James King argues that the John Hughes classic serves as proof "of how much easier the middle class have it" (294). This is evident not only by juxtaposing Ferris with Principal Rooney, but also by juxtaposing Ferris with characters from other iconic Hughes movies. Each of these representations demonstrates the privilege acquired when one has money and material markers of it.

According to King, Ferris could have been "soul brothers" with Duckie, a character from another Hughes movie, 1986's *Pretty in Pink*. Both Ferris and Duckie are quirky and idealistic; both could be described as outsiders. Ferris, however, is the outsider-insider, because unlike Duckie, he is loved by nearly everyone, which is made abundantly clear throughout the entire movie. Upon closer examination, the primary difference, the only difference, between these two characters is that Duckie lives (literally) on the wrong side of the tracks, and Ferris lives in an affluent suburb outside of Chicago (King,

294). In other words, Duckie is poor and Ferris has money; this difference ultimately translates to "a startling gap in self-confidence between the settled and suburban Ferris and the hard-up and nervy Duckie" (King, 294). Neither movie explores *why* each character belongs to their respective socioeconomic classes. Despite brief references to their parents' work, there is no mention of other social or political factors that influence their socioeconomic class. According to Dustin Kidd, author of *Popular Culture Freaks: Identify, Mass Media, and Society*, this is common in popular culture, particularly films, as "fluctuations or the levels of privilege and opportunity" are rarely discussed (80). Even though the reasons for Ferris's socioeconomic privilege remain relatively unexplained, viewers very much see the result of it.

Throughout the entire movie, Ferris is showered with peer approval, being able to do what he pleases when he pleases. The same cannot be said for Duckie. For example, when Duckie serenades Andie she is annoyed, but when Ferris serenades Sloane the entire city of Chicago celebrates (King, 294). Ferris's life highlights what it was like to live in an upper-middle-class lifestyle during the 1980s. Ferris gets the girl; Duckie does not. (In the original ending, Duckie was supposed to win over Andie, but the ending didn't test well with audiences.) Filmmakers believed most audiences would want to see Andie, who was also poor, end up with someone who could "save her" from poverty—rather fitting in a culture that promotes conspicuous consumption.

As noted, there is also a stark contrast between Ferris and Principal Rooney, and this juxtaposition provides yet another example of socioeconomic class and privilege. In *Ferris Bueller's Day Off*, the entire movie is a nod to consumption and excess, demonstrating how consumption equals peer approval and peer approval encourages more consumption. Ferris, Cameron, and Sloane skip school and traipse around Chicago in a very rare Ferrari owned by Cameron's father. The car is so rare, as Cameron repeatedly notes, it is only one of one hundred made. Before the trio commits to taking Cameron's father's car, Cameron offers an alternative mode of transportation—one that is costly in its own right. He suggests to Ferris they rent a "nice Cadillac" (*Ferris Bueller's Day Off*). To suggest this demonstrates a certain level of socioeconomic privilege; while not a rare Ferrari, in the 1980s Cadillacs were a symbol of wealth in the United States and had been for decades, particularly for older Americans (Stern). Ferris's own socioeconomic status is later confirmed when we see his dad driving an Audi, and his sister, who is also in high school, driving a new 1985 Pontiac Fiero (Hurlin). Even though Ferris doesn't have a car (he notes how he "asked for a car but got a computer"), the audience gets the impression that a car is likely in his future, and if it isn't, it is because of something Ferris did to disobey parents—not for a lack of money (*Ferris Bueller's Day Off*).

This is a stark contrast to their pursuer, Principal Rooney. Rooney drives a modest Plymouth Reliant, commonly known as a K-Car, a car that could be purchased in the early 1980s for as low as $7,235 depending on the options ("The K Car"). To further demonstrate his lower socioeconomic class, after his car gets towed, Rooney is forced to ride a school bus that brandishes one final degrading and disrespectful blow: "Rooney eats it" (*Ferris Bueller's Day Off*). In the 1980s, riding a school bus when the rider is of driving age marks the rider with a certain stigma. It simply is not considered cool; rich kids drive, poor kids ride the bus. As for adults, they drive—period. This is just one example, as Rooney is humiliated time and time again throughout the movie, highlighting his low socioeconomic status.

In regard to consumption, money is of no consequence for the teenagers. They cruise along Lake Shore Drive, attend a Chicago Cubs baseball game, visit the Art Institute of Chicago, and dine at an upscale restaurant. There is very little discussion how entrance to each of these activities is purchased. Some viewers might argue that Ferris is incredibly self-absorbed, and to some extent they would be right. At first glance, Ferris seems to only care about having fun and spending money; he doesn't seem to care whether or not he gets Cameron in trouble or causes his parents to worry. This behavior was noted by moviegoers and critics alike. Upon the movie's release, columnist George Will called Ferris a symptom of "the self-absorption of youth corrupted by the complacency of the Reagan years." Like many Gen Xers, however, Ferris is more complicated than what viewers like Will see on the surface. They are a series of contradictions, individualistic yet part of a larger, close-knit group.

Interestingly, as Principal Rooney searches for the teens, he looks for them not at these expensive landmarks but at local teen hangouts. Like the economics teacher featured at the beginning of the movie, this is yet another example of how out-of-touch the educational system is, if we view Rooney as a symbol of it. As an institutional pillar, time and time again Rooney is made to look like a fool by Gen Xers, living in excess and shirking their roles within the institution he is desperately trying to uphold. Additionally, the juxtaposition also demonstrates the rise of materialism and consumption in the 1980s, showing how Gen X very much participated.

Within the dataset, we see a similar contrast between another materialistic Gen Xer and institutional representative, Claire and Principal Vernon in *The Breakfast Club*. When the movie begins, Claire, sitting in her father's BMW, complains about her Saturday of detention. She is frustrated that she won't be able to go shopping as she originally planned and that her dad was unable or unwilling to get her out of detention. Her tone implies that her father usually has the power to do so, but decided against it because he is trying (although failing) to hold Claire accountable for her actions. Along with numerous aesthetic markers of the family's wealth (nice car, exquisite jewelry, and expensive food), this suggests that with money comes a certain amount of power. This is one of the only references within the 1980s dataset that suggests the interconnected relationship between economic class and social/political power. Any critique, however, is limited, as the remainder of the movie, like *Ferris Bueller's Day Off*, focuses on the possessions owned by both characters. For lunch, Claire, in her diamonds, eats sushi while Principal Vernon eats a traditional bag lunch, lamenting the state of youth (*The Breakfast Club*). Claire is contrasted not only with Principal Vernon but also with other detention-goers like Allison, who eats white bread and sugary cereal for lunch.

Ultimately, Ferris and Claire seem happy; although there are a few times in which Claire expresses some grief. Even these complaints, however, feel like shallow problems compared to the problems of her peers. In an attempt to garner sympathy from them, Claire states, "Do you know how popular I am? I am so popular. Everybody loves me so much at this school" (*The Breakfast Club*). During this scene, Claire tries to explain how difficult it is to be the center of attention. Claire argues that, unlike the rest of them, she is under an immense amount of pressure to perform. Yet, to others, her life appears worry-free. At least from an economic standpoint, her life appears to be much easier than the others in detention. She appears to be happy. Like representations of imperfect nuclear families, viewers see how money does not necessarily equate to happiness.

While it may make aspects of life easier, it doesn't guarantee fulfilling, healthy relationships.

In *Back to the Future* we see another representation of how money (and the stuff money can buy) is used in an attempt to secure familial happiness. After Marty travels back in time, his actions change the future. From a family perspective, after his time travel, things are much better. The family is much closer to the "ideal." They have good jobs and nice things, and George and Lorraine are frisky. Biff, the series antagonist, works for George. Beyond the aesthetics and traditional symbols of success (nice house, new furniture, expensive cars), the biggest thing that changes is personal fulfillment. In this version of their life, Marty's family is self-confident and wealthy as opposed to downtrodden and poor. Pre–time travel George never realizes his potential. Post–time travel George, however, finds it by knocking Biff out, and follows his [American Bootstraps] Dream of becoming an author. Crispin Glover, the actor who played George, was so upset with the message the film was propagating—that money equals happiness—he did not appear in the sequel (King, 242). Despite featuring Huey Lewis's "The Power of Love," the movie suggests that the power of money is what is needed to be happy—a theme absent in *Stranger Things*. The next section explores how *Stranger Things* depicts consumption, namely to what degree the series promotes the belief that money equals happiness.

Time for a Montage

In the first two seasons of *Stranger Things* there is less obvious consumption than in the 1980s dataset. Consumption is more implicit, with a focus on suburbia and what comes with living there: nice houses with picket fences, cars, and numerous possessions. As noted in chapter 2, there is a stark contrast between how the boys live due to the socioeconomic classes of their families: the Wheelers live in town on revered Maple Lane, while the Byers family live on the outskirts. These representations highlight what each family can and cannot afford. Throughout the series, popular culture artifacts are not only a symbol of parental substitution, but also materialism. While we see an array of popular culture items throughout the boys' bedrooms, and these possessions undoubtedly cost money, the cost of these possessions is never addressed. As noted in chapter 2, Gen X's relationship with popular culture—as babysitter and friend—reinforces both its importance *and* the belief that material goods are linked to happiness.

One of the primary locations of Season Three is the new local mall in Hawkins. In the 1980s malls were wildly popular and the ultimate symbol of 1980s consumption. In episode two Max takes Eleven to the mall and encourages her to "find herself" there. During a montage, Madonna's "Material Girl" plays while Eleven tries on clothes; this scene, echoing many 1980s movies featuring mall montages (*Night of the Comet* and *National Lampoon's European Vacation*), provides the most overt example of materialism in the series to date. As Eleven tries on neon-colored shirt after neon-colored shirt, Madonna sings, "'Cause we are living in a material world / And I am a material girl" ("Material Girl"). The song, wildly popular at the time, celebrates consumption. On one hand, in this scene it is great to see Max encourage Eleven to pursue interests and develop relationships beyond her relationship with Mike, a criticism of Eleven's character in earlier seasons. On the other hand, it is unfortunate that Max suggests Eleven focus on material goods to accomplish these goals. It implies that the way to find oneself, to define oneself, is via conspicuous consumption. While problematic, the scene feels authentic to the time period, given the rise of conspicuous consumption in 1980s culture with the mall as its centerpiece. In many ways, the mall is more than a location in *Stranger Things*; it is another primary character.

In the 1980s malls proliferated across the country, and for many Americans, especially teenagers, malls became a second home. Malls provided an opportunity for people to gather in close proximity with one another, an answer to the isolation associated with the suburban sprawl (Bogost). For a brief period of time in the 1980s, malls became America's cultural and social hubs. Because of their popularity, they also gave rise to micro-cultures (mallrats and mall walkers) and a micro movie genre (*Fast Times at Ridgemont High*, *Weird Science*, and *Night of the Comet*). Malls were so popular they nearly decimated small local businesses across the country. Many, however, are now abandoned, serving as a symbol of hard economic times and a change in consumer habits, e.g., online shopping.

The mall is a perfect reflection of 1980s economics and culture. As noted by Sophie Gilbert in *The Atlantic*, the setting of Season Three demonstrates how a "free-market economic system can be both impossibly damaging to small businesses (see: the new arrival of the Starcourt Mall in Hawkins) and a preferable alternative to the authoritarian communism of America's 1980s enemies." Despite concerns regarding the loss of culture, which is explored later in this chapter, Gen Xers very much participated in the proliferation of malls and subsequent downtown decay, abandoning mom and pop stores as they flocked to the mall in droves.

In Season Three of *Stranger Things*, downtown decay is apparent. The mall has nearly destroyed downtown Hawkins as well as local farmland around it. This is reminiscent of the mall in *Back to the Future*, as it occupied land that was once a residential area. In both the series and the movie, the vastness and the consequences of suburban sprawl is explored. Like so many felt in the 1980s, Nancy argues that the mall was "changing the fabric" of their existence ("Chapter One: Suzie, Do You Copy?"). Additionally, in *Stranger Things* Russians own the mall, using it to cover up their nefarious activity in Hawkins. Blind to how awful his backyard deal with the Russians really is, the mayor tells Hopper the mall's success is just "good old American capitalism" ("Chapter Two: The Mall Rats"). Russians using American values to undermine the well-being of America's heartland suggests that one of the very symbols of the country's existence and culture is its vulnerability. The mall is both a celebration of culture and a weakness. The next section explores how the 1980s dataset articulates the dangers of conspicuous consumption and a capitalistic system that privileges some and oppresses others.

Within some of the 1980s dataset, unbridled consumption is linked to waning community health and cultural loss, such as the loss of small businesses and the loss of fine art. Additionally, this consumption is also linked to the corruption and/or eroding of both formal and informal institutions, causing relationships to erode between Gen Xers and institutional agents. I conclude the section by examining how this paradox (concern and cynicism, yet unbridled participation) is nearly omitted in all seasons of *Stranger Things*.

Down and Out in Paradise:
Sacrificing Culture for Consumption

Samuelson notes that the 1980s saw employment rise by 18 million but low-skill labor (e.g., Joyce in *Stranger Things*)

experienced a relative wage loss. Wages failed to pace inflation, and according to Behr, living standards decreased by 16
percent throughout the decade. Throughout the 1980s dataset, the dangers of a system that privileges some and oppresses
others is explored. For example, in both *Back to the Future* and
Back to the Future II, in time travel time there is an even greater
schism between socioeconomic classes and strain on a variety of institutions. In *Back to the Future II*, as a result of this
schism, there is a loss of education (the local school is burned
down), and interpersonal relationships between family members are increasingly strained. Additionally, there is an uptick
in violence and corruption, and the environment is depleted in
both versions of the future. In the future newspaper that Doc
and Marty use as a barometer for their time-traveling success,
a headline reads MAN KILLED BY FALLING LITTER (*Back to
the Future II*). This motif is also seen in the first movie of the
trilogy during time travel; after time travel, the park is full of
trash, suggesting lack of civic funds or infrastructure. We also
see a homeless man sitting on a bench, particularly surprising
in a small town like Hill Valley, suggesting a level of economic
failure in the community. In both movies, we also see just how
closely the economy is intertwined with other American institutions such as family, education, and government. I discuss the
latter representation in more detail in chapter 4, specifically
Gen X's response to government officials and agents.

Vanishing Cultural Health

Not only does this unequal system threaten the physical health
of a community (the education, safety, and health of its residents), but the movies within the 1980s dataset suggest that it
also threatens the *cultural* health of a community. There is no

greater example of this than in *Gremlins*. At the beginning of *Gremlins*, the Chinese grandfather warns the American father who wants to purchase a sacred Chinese creature as a gift for his son: "You do with mogwai what your society . . . has done with all of nature's gifts. You do not understand" (*Gremlins*). This exchange highlights the belief that the implied gifts of the East—such as nature—cannot be trusted by those in the West in the wake of unyielding capitalism and, more specifically, 1980s materialism and conspicuous consumption. Throughout the dataset *(E.T. the Extra-Terrestrial, Nightmare on Elm Street, Stranger Things)*, we see that comfortable suburban environments do not protect individuals from the dangers both outside and within. This is true in *Gremlins*, as the whole town—regardless of socioeconomic class—is overtaken by destructive little monsters mindlessly consuming mindless popular culture.

Other plot points in *Gremlins* suggest that cultural health, in the age of materialism, is fleeting. The teenagers work to declare the local pub a historical landmark to prevent the bank from tearing it down, but it seems like an insurmountable feat, given the bank's unyielding power in the community. Similarly, in both *Back to the Future* and *Back to the Future II*, citizens of Hill Valley fundraise to save the beloved and historical clock tower, despite the mayor—in future time—wanting to tear it down. In both *Gremlins* and *Back to the Future*, ordinary citizens are fighting much larger forces that seek to abolish cultural artifacts. For example, throughout *Gremlins* different people complain about, and have conflict with, the bank. While the issue with the bank and the growing gremlin population seem like two completely different issues, both point to the same message: greed and consumption are the demise of sleepy little towns. For example, as the gremlins tear through the town, they binge on current popular culture. Their binge is what fosters and proliferates their destruction. Anthony Scibelli explains:

> *Gremlins* is easily read as an inverse of *E.T.* Spielberg celebrates the potential of media as a means to instruct and educate: E.T. learns to speak by watching *Sesame Street* and concocts his plan to reach home by reading a Buck Rogers comic strip. The Gremlins love media too, but only for its pure entertainment value. They act out scenes from *Flashdance* and *Phantom of the Opera*, and they mindlessly watch *Snow White*, singing along to the asinine music in a violent celebration. (Scibelli)

In the midst of 1980s excess, the message suggests that *mindless* consumption, particularly mindless consumption of *mindless* popular culture, leads to obliteration of communities and their culture.

This subtext of *Gremlins* reflects the 1980s film industry as a whole. The industry was significantly changed by the 1980s economy, ultimately contributing to the loss of culture while simultaneously creating it. Conglomerates were formed, film budgets ballooned, and consumer exploitation proliferated (movie-themed products and product placement) (McWilliams). During this decade, much like the economy as a whole, the film industry's profits were the highest in industry history. These record-breaking profits, however, "were ominous for film as art, since they emphasize entertainment values over artistic ones and they enforce conformity and conservatism" (McWilliams, 100). The money was often only seen by a few—and not the creators. Just as the gremlins' media consumption left the town in shambles, the changes in the film industry left independent artists in shambles.

We also see this trope, the fear of cultural loss, in *The Goonies*. Mikey and Brand's father is a museum curator, and when asked what his father will do with the artifacts in the attic upon the demolition of the house, Mikey says he will probably give them back to the museum or, if he is able, to the new curator. While it is clear that his father is most worried about his family and the loss of their home, he is also worried about the loss of community culture, as he saw himself as a gatekeeper of sorts. The boys also express great concern and doubt; would someone appreciate and care for the artifacts as much as their father had? The children are not so sure.

Despite these very real fears that excess was threatening art, materialism flourished and support for unbridled capitalism grew, including within the Gen X community. This is depicted throughout the 1980s dataset and Season Three of *Stranger Things*. Community and cultural health is not overtly addressed in the first two seasons of *Stranger Things*; the focus remains more on familial health, as I discuss in chapter 2. Throughout the entire series, however, the Duffer brothers suggest that possessions do not make a happy family (unlike the McFlys in *Back to the Future*); in fact, sometimes they can get in the way of happiness. In Season Three, the widening income gap, and a system that privileges some and oppresses others, are highlighted. One poignant exchange between Murray and Alexei summarizes the Duffer brothers' message. While at the local Fourth of July fair, Murray tells Alexei: "It doesn't get more American than *this*, my friend—fatty foods, ugly decadence, rigged games.... They have been designed to present the illusion of fairness! But it's all a scam, a trick, to put your money in the rich man's pocket. That, my dear friend, is *America*" ("Chapter Seven: The Bite").

In this scene, the ugly underbelly of the United States is illustrated. The exchange between Murray and Alexei highlights how unrealistic the American Dream is for many Americans: despite how hard they work, they will never achieve economic advancement because the system itself is rigged. Murray explains how the whole concept of the American Dream is built on bias and privileges the rich much like the rigged games at the fair. In Season Three, for example, we also see what the mall has done to downtown Hawkins, suggesting not only unfairness but also a level of cultural loss, the same unfairness and loss to which Murray alludes.

Throughout the 1980s, the rise of consumption also reinforced individualism. This individualism led to a more conservative view of the American Dream, even for those who did not have much. This time period fostered a unique perspective, the desire to be an individual but also part of a group. In the next section I discuss how those affected by the widening income gap embraced individualism and fought back, questioning the American Dream.

Right Now (It's Your Tomorrow): Gen X Taking Back What Is Theirs

For those families who were stunted by Reagan's policies, a "taking back what is mine" attitude developed, which is most visible in *The Goonies*. For example, the children come across a wishing well and think it is the pirate treasure. In this instance, the wishing well represents the antithesis of wish fulfillment. Mikey thinks he found the treasure; instead, he found a bunch of loose change. However, the boys are told they cannot take what little money is there because to do so represents taking/stealing someone else's wishes and dreams. Mouth replies, "Yeah. But ya know what? This one. This one right here [holding up a coin].

This was my dream, my wish. It didn't come true. I'm takin' it back. I'm takin' 'em all back" (*The Goonies*). Mouth's comment is a cynical critique of the then current economic climate, echoing Gen X's "I am taking back what is mine" attitude. This scene highlights how, for many, the American Dream is a false narrative; it demonstrates how Americans were told to buy into an idea that simply does not exist. Ultimately, it shows that just because people work hard does not mean they will find success and wealth.

For Mikey, finding the treasure and saving his family home truly seems like an impossible dream, a myth. *The Goonies* reflects this theme via the narrative of buried treasure; in real life, Americans search for their "treasure" in get-rich-quick venues, such as the lottery and game shows, because the American Dream of hard work and thrift is no longer a reality (Warshauer). Yet, like the Byers family in *Stranger Things*, those in *The Goonies* most down on their luck celebrate family and strong familial relationships. At the end of the movie, Mikey laments the fact that he was unable to find the treasure. He states, "If I found one-eyed Willy's rich stuff, I'd pay all of my dad's bills. Then maybe he'd get to sleep at night instead of sitting up, trying to figure out a way for all of us to stay here" (*The Goonies*). After thinking he lost the treasure, Mikey apologizes to his father. His father, however, reassures him, saying that having their children safe "makes us the richest people in Astoria" (*The Goonies*). While this message is sweet, reflecting close familial bonds, it is here, in Mikey's response, we also see the pessimism that often plagues Gen X; unlike previous generations, class mobility for many is all but nonexistent.

As mentioned previously, in Season Three of *Stranger Things* townspeople are concerned about the dwindling downtown business not just for economic purposes but for cultural ones as well. As Nancy argued, the mall (and the struggling down-town) was changing their town in dramatic ways. The mayor conversely urges Hopper to deal with those concerned, namely those concerned with the mall's impact on small businesses. When Hopper recommends the mayor allow the protesters to speak their minds, the mayor scoffs. He snidely replies that they will soon forget about the mall and his misdeeds, as he is planning a large Fourth of July celebration. He tells Hopper that after the celebration, "That's all voters will remember" ("Chapter Two: The Mall Rats"). This is a reflection of the eco-nomic climate at the time and how many Gen Xers viewed the government and its officials as untrustworthy, snide, and self-serving. This attitude is explored in greater detail in chapter 4.

Under Pressure: Trapped in an Economic Paradox

There is a famous line in *Ferris Bueller's Day Off* that adequately summarizes Gen X's view toward the economy and the govern-ment in general. When referencing his history test, Ferris states: "European socialism. I mean, really, what's the point? I'm not European. I don't plan on being European. So who gives a crap if they're socialists? They could be fascist anarchists—it still wouldn't change the fact that I don't own a car" (*Ferris Bueller's Day Off*). Ferris's perspective highlights two key points, both of which reflect Gen X attitudes at the time. First and foremost, Ferris is generally tolerant of others and diverse viewpoints. We see this not only in the above comment but also throughout the entire movie. Ferris is nice to everyone, except, of course, his adversary, Principal Rooney. Generally speaking, Gen X is known for this tolerance, as they "tend to be much more sym-pathetic to individuals and groups historically marginalized by society" (Watson, xvi). While individualistic, Gen Xers also generally welcome diverse perspectives.

Second, Ferris is primarily concerned with his own well-being and is generally disinterested in economics, politics, and world affairs. As I note throughout this chapter and discuss in more detail in chapter 4, this attitude reflects the attitudes of many teenagers throughout time, regardless of generation. This is particularly true of Gen Xers. Ted Halstead writes: "A wide sampling of surveys indicates that Xers are less politically or civically engaged, exhibit less social trust or confidence in government, have a weaker allegiance to their country or to either political party, and are more materialistic than their predecessors." This lack of allegiance or patriotism is seen throughout the movie, and this position is not unique to Ferris. In one of the most often quoted lines of the 1980s, Ferris states, "A person should not believe in an -ism, he should believe in himself" (*Ferris Bueller's Day Off*). This line itself highlights the paradox of the 1980s for many Gen Xers; while the quote *suggests* cynicism in the economy and the government, it also highlights the *primary* underlying principle of capitalism: consumption and individualism.

In many ways the 1980s was a paradox. Andersen, for example, characterizes this time period as manic (e.g., engaging in "pleasurable activities that have a high potential for painful consequences," such as "unrestrained buying sprees, or foolish business investments)." In other words, the 1980s highlighted the contradictory nature of mixed states. America was not alone in her manic episodes; as seen in *Ferris Bueller's Day Off*, many Gen Xers' viewpoints on the economy and consumption were a mixed bag, both complex and contradictory. In the early 1980s, after the implementation of Reagan's deregulation and cuts to social programs, Americans faced a recession. Many faced economic instability causing great concern, specifically regarding unemployment and the ballooning federal budget deficit (Auxier). This caused doubt on how quickly (or if at all) the economy would recover. Richard Auxier, research associate for the Urban-Brookings Tax Policy Center, writes, "A September 1983 Gallup poll found that three-fourths of the public agreed that the federal government's budget deficit was a great threat (42%) or somewhat of a threat (34%) to the continuing recovery of the economy." As the income gap continued to widen, Americans had less and less confidence in their elective officials. Some Gen Xers saw their parents struggle and soon felt the economic pinch themselves.

This general uneasiness fostered feelings of distrust among Americans, specifically Gen Xers. Distrust in the economy and in government officials grew. While some (largely upper-class) families profited from early 1980s economic policies, other families struggled as wages failed to pace inflation. As noted in this chapter, this ultimately widened the income gap. It is logical that this gap would be explored throughout much of 1980s popular culture, including the 1980s dataset. It also is present in *Stranger Things*. Despite economic uncertainty, however, the "manic" 1980s ushered in a new, more materialistic culture. Rather than saving during uncertain times, Americans spent. In the search of happiness and prestige, Americans opened their pocketbooks lined with plastic. During the mid-1980s, conspicuous consumption, including self-gifting, was on the rise, a sign of a culture shifting toward materialism (McKeage).

While the economy eventually began to recover, the income gap remained stretched. This did not deter Xers, however, from continuing to spend. The culture transitioned to one that celebrated not just consumption but conspicuous consumption, motivated by wanting to display one's economic power and prestige (Veblen). The era was characterized by "the giddy obsession with markets and money, racking up debt, spending instead of saving" (Andersen). This obsession heavily influenced popular culture both within the 1980s dataset (*Big, Ferris Bueller's Day Off*, and *The Breakfast Club*) as well as outside of it (*Wall Street, Say Anything*, and *Pretty in Pink*). In these movies we see income inequality via visual representation. However, materialism also increased the number of movies that depicted the struggles of Americans who were threatened by economic development and consumption, unable to participate themselves, including *The Goonies* and *Gremlins*. Some movies, such as *The Breakfast Club*, represented both perspectives, ultimately demonstrating the tension between the haves and the have-nots, serving as micro-level examination of what was happening in the country. These representations suggested that the American Dream was much harder to achieve than initially thought.

As most were coming of age during this time, Gen X was not immune to the turmoil festering from within the country, which ultimately helped foster a deep-rooted cynicism. Yet, despite Gen X's mistrust in the economy, they were very much participants, giving rise to the "material girls" and "yuppies" (a derogatory term coined for 1980s young urban professionals with disposable income), although many people being labeled yuppies were actually late Baby Boomers. This is particularly true in the mid- to late 1980s, as unemployment dropped and the economy recovered slowly. This is reflected within the 1980s dataset and to a lesser extent in *Stranger Things*. While some 1980s popular culture celebrated this behavior, other popular culture, including some within the 1980s dataset, was quick to warn of the dangers of unyielding capitalism, namely, the depletion of community and cultural health. This is particularly noticeable in the *Back to the Future* series.

In Seasons One and Two of *Stranger Things*, the critique of unyielding capitalism diverges slightly from the 1980s dataset. We see less consumption overall, and when we do it is accompanied by an implicit social critique of how this behavior is intertwined with the health of a variety of institutions: family, education, and government. Perhaps the greatest focus, as noted earlier, is how the economy (and consumption) intersects with, and can strain, familial relationships. In Season Three, however, the setting is the very symbol of 1980s materialism: the mall. The site, we see, brings both pleasure and pain to each of the characters.

Finally, just as I cannot talk about family without talking about the economy, I cannot talk about the economy without talking about the government. The focus of chapter 4 is Gen X's growing cynicism toward the government and government authorities from the local level to the national. This, of course, was fostered by decisions regarding the economy, but it goes much deeper. Throughout the 1980s dataset and *Stranger Things*, from the local level to the national level, Gen Xers seeking assistance are continually dismissed. This dismissal strained relationships, relationships with the legal and penal systems that had already been damaged. These relationships, namely with authority figures within those systems, are discussed in chapter 4.

—4—
Fight the Power
Gen X's Relationship with the Law and Government

In the 1980s there was a sense that, beneath the political and economic veneer, the country was vulnerable, from the outside as well as from the inside. This vulnerability seemingly stuck with Gen Xers, who witnessed a series of tragedies in their lifetimes and the government's response to them. Journalist Rob Owen explains how these experiences fostered skepticism in Gen Xers: "Xers have seen news footage of dozens of airplane crashes, the space shuttle explosion, the bombing of the World Trade Center and the Oklahoma City Federal Building, and still people wonder why Xers are unwilling to trust their elders, the government, and even each other" (55). In the early to mid-1980s, government officials, including President Reagan, exacerbated these fears in the hope of convincing Americans they/he could dissipate them. These actions had profound impact on impressionable young Gen Xers.

During his 1984 reelection campaign, Reagan encouraged voters to go back to a safer, more wholesome time via his now infamous and award-winning "Morning in America" commercial. The commercial features white, small-town Americans engaging in 1950s *Leave It to Beaver* behaviors (Smokler). The ad suggests that upon his 1980 election, and "after 20 years of social tumult, assassinations, riots, scandal, an unpopular war and gas lines, Mr. Reagan returned the United States to the tranquility of the 1950s" (Beschloss). For voters who were struggling from both a social and economic perspective, the message was appealing. Many voters overlooked how some of Reagan's first-term economic policies caused or exacerbated the turmoil they were experiencing.

As noted by presidential historian Michael Beschloss, the ad's "haze of nostalgia and optimism helped obscure Mr. Reagan's lingering political problems with the deficit and unemployment." Walter Mondale, Reagan's 1984 Democratic opponent, critiqued the ad: "It's all picket fences and puppy dogs. No one's hurting. No one's alone. No one's hungry. No one's unemployed. No one gets old. Everybody's happy" (Beschloss). Despite Mondale's justified criticisms, and the noted racist undertones of the ad itself (there were no obvious people of color featured in the minute-long spot), the ad was widely popular and helped elect Reagan to a second term, in small part because of Gen X. In 1984, while a small percentage of the total vote (11 percent), 61 percent of 18–24-year-olds voted for Reagan, while 39 percent of 18–24-year-olds voted for Mondale ("How Groups Voted"). While it may seem odd that the generation branded as slackers would vote for the conservative ticket, there were some early indicators that suggested Gen Xers were likely to support Reagan.

Howe and Strauss note that as young adults, the emerging political agenda of Gen Xers interested in politics was to "make simple things work again," and Reagan's campaign addressed that message (*13th Gen*, 163). Gen Xers who voted for Reagan were able to look past the ongoing economic uncertainty outlined in chapter 3 on the promise of a better, simpler tomorrow. This is not to say that Reagan met these expectations during his two terms as president. In chapter 5, I examine in detail how Reagan's election and administration, and the elections and administrations of subsequent presidents, further shaped Gen X, particularly in regard to their perceptions of the economy and government. In general, however, over the years Gen Xers have been skeptical of politicians and politics, and Reagan was not immune to their wariness.

The economic difficulties faced by Gen Xers continued despite Reagan's reelection, as warned by his opponents and critics, ultimately serving as fuel for Gen Xers' growing pessimism and apathy. For many Gen Xers, economic difficulties heightened their distrust in government and elected officials, including Reagan himself. Gen Xers observed how once-trusted institutions were abandoning their generation. Ted Halstead, contributor to *The Atlantic*, writes about the 1980s and coming-of-age Gen Xers:

> Xers are facing a particularly acute economic insecurity, which leads them to turn inward and pursue material well-being above all else. They see the outlines of very real problems ahead—fiscal, social, and environmental. But in the nation's political system they perceive no leadership on the issues that concern them; rather, they see self-serving politicians who continually indenture themselves to the highest bidders. So Xers have decided, for now, to tune out.

Some Gen Xers' response to this economic uncertainty was to disengage from politics altogether, believing that the "basic fabric of American society" was "somehow fraying" (Halstead). For example, many apathetic Gen Xers believed there was no reason to participate in the political process after noting how more and more policies favored the elderly. These same Gen Xers also noticed how politicians spoke negatively about their age group, creating a greater disconnect between them and both major political parties. When they did participate, including the 1984 election, Gen Xers cultivated "an attitude of political reaction" (Howe and Strauss, *13th Gen*, 164). In other words, if a political party or elected officials were no longer keeping its/their promises, Gen Xers were happy to look elsewhere or even choose not to choose, refraining from voting altogether. This was most evident in the 1992 election of William Jefferson Clinton (Howe and Strauss, *13th Gen*, 164), as Gen Xers overwhelming voted for Democratic candidate Clinton, breaking a twelve-year Republican hold on the office.

As a result of their political abstention and/or political fluidity, "savvy, skeptical and self-reliant" (Taylor and Gao) Gen Xers garnered a reputation for putting trust in themselves and those closest to them. They came to rely on their personal networks, rather than institutions, for support. Peter Hanson, author of *The Cinema of Generation X: A Critical Study of Films and Directors*, writes, "Because Gen Xers, speaking in the most general terms, aren't tethered to family and other institutions in the ways that their predecessors were, they create a comforting cocoon of artifice" (43). Many Gen Xers prefer to put their trust in one another and not in institutions, such as political parties, that they believe will sooner or later disappoint them (Howe and Strauss, *13th Gen*, 164).

Throughout the 1980s dataset, we see several representations that *seem* to evoke the spirit of Reagan's "Morning in America" commercial, namely *Back to the Future* and *Dead Poets Society*.

Undoubtedly, it is no surprise that one of Reagan's favorite movies was *Back to the Future*, likely because of its surface-level romanticizations of yesteryear and nod to the American Dream. A former Reagan speechwriter, Mark Weinberg, recalled watching the movie with Reagan, noting how Reagan resembled Doc Brown's tenaciousness. Weinberg also noted how Reagan believed the movie was "the type of movie that Hollywood should be making, as opposed to some of the more controversial, violent or adult-themed films that seemed all too common at the time." Because he enjoyed the movie so much, Reagan even quoted it in his 1986 State of the Union address, proclaiming, "Never has there ever been a more exciting time to be alive, a time of rousing wonder and heroic achievement. As they said in the film *Back to the Future*, where we are going, we don't need roads." In 1989, *Back to the Future II* referenced Reagan's "Morning in America" commercial, during one of Marty's time-travel scenes. This scene was not a sign of mutual admiration, however. It was more of a chance to poke fun at Reagan and his administration.

In *Back to the Future II*, Marty travels to the future and enters a 1980s-themed cafe. Upon entering the establishment, a robot greets him. The robot, a talking head on a television screen, resembles Reagan. The robot states, "Welcome to the Cafe '80s, where it's always Morning in America, even in the afternoo-noo-noon" (*Back to the Future II*). Upon closer inspection, viewers will notice that Cafe '80s is not a realistic representation of the 1980s; rather, it is a bizarre, hyperbolic depiction of the decade. This depiction clearly pokes fun of the function of nostalgia, including the slice of nostalgia sold by Reagan in the "Morning in America" commercial.

While the *Back to the Future* trilogy and *Dead Poets Society* offer a WASP-y, rose-colored vision of a fantasized normative

America, like Cafe '80s, they do so as a means to critique overly romanticized representations of the past. When one watches these movies closely, there are clear cracks in the façade of perfection. In *Dead Poets Society*, for example, things look "perfect," but an ugly reality resided within, including troubled nuclear families and a fraught private school. Additionally, in these movies it is clear that children and teens cannot rely on authority figures for assistance or protection.

During Gen X's childhood, according to Howe and Strauss, there were also numerous movies made featuring vigilante justice; these movies featured ordinary people fighting violent offenders that were unjustly let loose into society (*13th Gen*, 125). Young Gen Xers saw violent crime go unpunished on television and in film, and this undoubtedly had an impact on their worldview. Additionally, young Gen Xers, who were frequently left home alone, were repeatedly warned by their parents of possible threats to their safety. As a result of being inundated with messages that crime was everywhere and that authority figures might not be there to help them when crime occurs, as adolescents Gen Xers learned to view "crime as an omnipresent threat to the already-fragile security of their lives and income" (Howe and Strauss, *13th Gen*, 125).

Indeed, the relationship between Gen Xers and law enforcement was fragile. White Gen Xers living in suburbia retained these messages in movies and music, while Gen Xers of color lived it, struggling to find common ground with police forces that were overwhelming white, and in some cases racist. These injustices were well documented in rap music, a genre gaining popularity in the early 1990s. Arguably, one of the most influential moments of Gen X's youth was the Rodney King beating and the riots that followed. In 1991, King, a construction worker, was the victim of police brutality captured on video. Like many Americans, Gen Xers saw, in real time, the effects of eroded relationships with police. They saw the effects of long-developed institutional racism. Throughout the 1980s dataset, this is one of the most salient themes to emerge: law enforcement dismissing and disappointing Gen Xers seeking assistance. No films within the dataset, however, address such serious issues as police abuse (as seen in the Rodney King beating and the subsequent LA riots). In 1980s popular culture, the focus was primarily to highlight authorities' ineptness. This is apparent within the 1980s dataset and outside of it as well (e.g., *Police Academy* and *Naked Gun*).

Within the 1980s dataset, viewers repeatedly see exchanges between Gen Xers and law enforcement that also illustrate an eroding, and sometimes toxic, relationship between the two parties. This erosion, in turn, confirms and strengthens Gen X's cynicism. Throughout the analyzed texts, authorities are regularly unreliable and, at times, painfully incompetent. Furthermore, in a few of the analyzed texts, authorities are outright dangerous—both unknowingly and knowingly. In a few extreme cases, government officials actually harm, in varying degrees, citizens seeking assistance, further eroding trust between agents of the government and Gen X.

In this chapter, I explore the ways in which the government and its agents are depicted within the 1980s dataset, namely through two primary representations: the unhelpful and incompetent police officer and the faceless, iniquitous government official. Both of these representations demonstrate and reinforce Gen X's cynicism toward the government, suggesting that the vision Reagan provided in his "Morning in America" commercial was far from reality for many coming-of-age Gen Xers. I also explore the ways in which *Stranger Things* draws upon these two representations. To some degree, both representations are seen in *Stranger Things*, albeit with slight variations. Unlike the 1980s dataset, one of the primary differences in the series is how some government officials are humanized and given opportunities for redemption. These moments of redemption are important as they tend to humanize not only the individual but also the institution the individual represents. Throughout *Stranger Things* we see positive relationships develop, however slowly, between government agents and Gen Xers, suggesting that a once strained relationship has been, or at least is capable of being, mended.

Mr. Policeman: The Dismissing of X

Throughout the 1980s dataset, there are several depictions of police officers who are dismissive of Gen Xers seeking assistance (*Gremlins*, *The Goonies*, and *Nightmare on Elm Street*). In each of these examples, the officers are unwilling to respond to pleas for assistance because they believe they know more than the young Gen Xers asking for help. This motif reflects an increasing anti-child sentiment in the country (e.g., the growing Zero Population Movement, a movement that supports holding the world's population constant) and in film (e.g., the growing number of movies featuring evil children). Howe and Strauss note the abundance of 1970s movies in which children are depicted as evil: *Rosemary's Baby*, *The Omen*, and *The Exorcist*. I argue that the "untrustworthy teen seeking assistance" trope is an extension of the evil child motif; it is another manifestation of the anti-child sentiment, and thus anti-Gen X, growing across the country (*13th Gen*, 63). While the Gen Xers seeking assistance within the 1980s dataset are not evil, they are viewed by law enforcement as posing just as much of a threat. This sentiment was noticed by Gen Xers who, in turn, became less trusting of authority figures.

As noted by Howe and Strauss, Gen Xers "perceived an outside world that does not like them" (*13th Gen*, 121). Throughout their childhood, they had come to view authority figures as unreliable. During their youth Gen Xers saw a shift in how youthful transgressions were discussed in the media and by authority figures such as politicians and law enforcement. When Baby Boomers were young, their crimes were often linked to "rage and betrayed expectations" (Howe and Strauss, *13th Gen*, 121). When Gen Xers were young, their crimes were seen as insensate and emotionally detached (Howe and Strauss, *13th Gen*, 121). According to Howe and Strauss, when teenage Baby Boomers got in trouble, they heard political leaders and law enforcement call for increased social services; but when teenage Gen Xers got in trouble, they heard political leaders and law enforcement officials call for "boot-camp prisons—or swift execution" (*13th Gen*, 45). During the 1970s, the amount of people incarcerated more than tripled, and the idea of rehabilitation was left behind. The message received by Gen Xers was clear: they were suspect, unwanted by many and, in some cases, not worthy of resources and rehabilitation. These messages and subsequent policies put additional strain on an already delicate relationship, causing Gen Xers' frustration with law enforcement to mount (Howe and Strauss, *13th Gen*, 121).

The next section will provide specific examples from the 1980s dataset and *Stranger Things*. My analysis points to numerous instances in which local law enforcement failed to help, or adequately help, Gen Xers seeking assistance; these examples both highlight and reinforce Gen X's attitude toward the government and its law enforcement agencies and agents. Additionally, in *Nightmare on Elm Street*, we see evidence of institutional corruption and decay, reflecting and reinforcing Gen X's increasing skepticism. Not only are government officials unable/unwilling to help; they are willing to profit at the expense of those they were hired to serve and protect, including vulnerable coming-of-age Gen Xers.

Exacerbating Disaster

In the 1980s dataset, in each instance, the officials' unwillingness to help exacerbates impending disasters. For example, in *Gremlins*, when Billy tries to warn the police of a growing gremlin population, he is told in condescending manner, "Go home and open your Christmas presents." Meanwhile, the gremlins continue to reproduce, terrorize, and destroy the entire town. In *The Goonies* the police are also depicted as inept and unhelpful. At the beginning of the movie, one of the jailed mafia members fakes suicide (and a very poor attempt at that) and is able to break out of jail because of how ineffectively the officer on duty responded. Later in the movie, when Chunk tries to explain that he is being held captive by said escaped (and known to local law enforcement) mafia members, the sheriff skeptically questions, "Is that you again, Lawrence?" (*The Goonies*).

In another example of incompetence, Ferris's sister, Jeanie, calls the police after she realizes there is an intruder in her house who, unbeknownst to her, is Principal Rooney. Rather than take her report and obvious distress seriously, the police arrest her for making a false police report. During the movie, we do not see them respond, question, or investigate; we only see Jeanie sitting in the police lobby waiting for her mother to pick her up. It is automatically assumed that she is not to be believed even though there was evidence of the break-in—Principal Rooney's forgotten wallet. In all of the above examples, the ineptness of local law enforcement is astounding and has dramatic consequences.

The most overt example of incompetence, however, is in *Nightmare on Elm Street*. It also has the gravest consequences. In this example, to make matters even more mind boggling, one of the police officers is the father of the Gen Xer seeking assistance. This situation reflects how both parents *and* law enforcement are unable to care for troubled Gen Xers because of their own shortcomings. *Nightmare on Elm Street* not only offers additional examples of strained parent-child relationships (as discussed in chapter 2) and bumbling and disbelieving police officers but also explores the dire consequences of a failed justice system. The movie chronicles the extreme actions ordinary people must take to fend off and protect themselves from evil forces when institutions are corrupt and/or deteriorate.

Throughout *Nightmare on Elm Street*, the police are unskilled and substandard, as serial killer Freddy stalks and kills local teenagers in their dreams. As opposed to other villains within the 1980s dataset, but like the shadow monster in *Stranger Things*, Freddy is the direct result of institutional failure. We learn that, nearly a decade prior to the current year of *Nightmare on Elm Street*, Freddy murdered approximately twenty children. Despite these horrific crimes, Freddy was acquitted on a technicality—an unsigned warrant. This entire plot reflects a failed system in two primary ways. First, Freddy is set free due to shoddy police work; if the warrant had been signed, we are led to believe he would have been convicted. Second, to make this situation even more heinous, the lawyers and judge involved in the case try—and do—profit from it. (How, exactly, is not explained in the movie.) This reinforces and reflects how Gen X was skeptical of all aspects of justice system, and not only in *Nightmare on Elm Street*. In *Back to the*

Future II, Marty discovers his son is going to be arrested and tried in only a matter of days. Doc notes, "The justice system works swiftly in the future now they have abolished lawyers" (*Back to the Future II*). This jab suggests it is lawyers who are responsible for prolonged trials (a problem), but also shows their importance in that, while Marty's son was not the primary instigator in the robbery, he shoulders the blame (what happens when the system goes unchecked).

Additionally, in *Nightmare on Elm Street*, townspeople are forced to engage in vigilante justice; we learn how distraught parents stalk Freddy after the botched trial, ultimately finding him and setting him on fire. This, however, is not the end of Freddy, as he now haunts and murders the teenagers of Springwood in their dreams. Just as the parents sought revenge, so does Freddy. Freddy's revenge is fueled by a faulty and eroded legal system, and Gen Xers are forced to pay the ultimate price: their lives. It is unsurprising that a movie within the dataset explores what it means to inherit problems created by previous generations, problems created and exasperated by inept local law enforcement and a failed legal system. As Halstead notes, Gen X is familiar with acquiring a wide array of problems as the result of institutional failures: "BESIDES struggling against downward economic mobility, Generation X is inheriting a daunting array of fiscal, social, and environmental debts." Specifically, on Elm Street the teenagers inherit the missteps and sins of the previous generation, and because of the mistakes made by the police, and the vigilante justice that followed, a vengeful Freddy roams free.

Like Nancy in *Nightmare on Elm Street*, other Gen Xers within the dataset are forced to confront evil and protect themselves as institutions and infrastructure fail around them. In fact, this is a common theme throughout the movies listed above. Without assistance, for example, Billy must fight the gremlins, and the children in *The Goonies* must fight the mafia and pirate ghosts. In each of these examples, there are varying degrees of institutional failure, but in each instance, one thing remains a constant: police only get involved when they can no longer deny there is an actual problem. Even when they do get involved sooner, they typically are not helpful, causing additional problems for Gen Xers. Seeing this on the large screen echoed and reinforced Gen Xers' feelings of being dismissed or belittled, ultimately affirming their distrust in authority.

We also see a similar motif in *Stranger Things*. As we learn in Season Two, the Upside Down world (parallel universe), and the shadow monster that resides there, are the result of a government experiment gone badly. The Gen X children must do what they can to save their friend and their town; unlike the movies discussed above, however, the children eventually work with local police and government officials to save their friend and their town. In fact, one of their greatest allies is Sheriff Hopper. This is a clear departure from its source material and will be discussed in greater detail later in the chapter. The next section, however, discusses how sometimes police work is not only shoddy but downright cruel.

Born in the USA: Inept and Cruel Officers and Agents

Most of the examples listed above outline mistakes made by law enforcement that were due to poor police work and patronizing attitudes (thinking they know more than the Gen Xers seeking assistance). Within the 1980s, there are other instances when law enforcement's mistakes are more serious, and in some cases the lack of assistance is purposeful and thus cruel. Within the 1980s dataset and *Stranger Things*, local law enforcement officials typically are seen as bumbling and/or skeptical. On the other hand, *national* law enforcement officials, and the government agencies they are associated with, are portrayed very differently. These officials and their respective agencies are typically faceless and are offered very few humanizing moments. They are mostly one-dimensional, mysterious figures that enact cruel policies on behalf of the US government. The next two sections will examine these representations, focusing most closely on *E.T. the Extra-Terrestrial* and *Stranger Things*. Unlike the 1980s dataset, *Stranger Things* offers both explicit and implicit examples of this representation.

Faceless Government Officials

In *E.T. the Extra-Terrestrial*, the federal agents are depicted as not only inept but also omnipresent and sinister. At one point in the movie, we see a "US Government" sign on a car, and in the very next shot, we see a faceless man holding a shotgun. This juxtaposition is meant to demonstrate the lengths to which government agents would go to get their way. Throughout the movie, there are countless, faceless government workers; they dress in astronaut suits, for example, and continually monitor the conversations of ordinary people. They lurk in seemingly quiet suburban neighborhoods. After one misstep from an average citizen, however, they descend upon the typically peaceful area, overwhelming the suburbanites with numbers and technology.

Yet, like the local law enforcement officials discussed earlier in this chapter, despite their sinister motives and their acts of cruelty, they are at times inept. Throughout *E.T. the Extra-Terrestrial*, while government officials are clearly heavily monitoring the Taylor household, they still manage to bungle capturing and retaining E.T. despite their weapons and surveillance measures. They barge into the home without care or consequence, as the mom helplessly proclaims, "This is MY home" (*E.T. the Extra-Terrestrial*). This proclamation reinforces that no place is safe, including one's own home, as danger comes from the outside and from within. The federal government agents' motives in *E.T.*, however, appear more sinister than the motives of local law enforcement officials in other movies within the dataset.

Once E.T. is captured and in failing health, Elliot is given the chance to say goodbye to him. During this scene, a scientist, presumably employed by the government, states, "I'm glad he met you first" (*E.T. the Extra-Terrestrial*). In this instance, we get the impression the scientist's allegiance is to science, not the government. This small comment is not insignificant, as it suggests that at least some government officials—although not law enforcement—are wary of their employer and the work they are being asked to do.

The next section outlines in greater detail how government officials are represented in *Stranger Things*. While there are parallels between the 1980s dataset and the series, including interactions with cruel scientists, the Duffer brothers do more to humanize government authorities by offering some of them moments of redemption—an amplified version of the *E.T.* scene with Elliot and the scientist.

Hit Me with Your Best Shot:
Distrust Running Deep in the Upside Down

In *Stranger Things*, distrust in authority runs deep, from the local level to the national. This distrust is not unsupported.

Like texts within the 1980s dataset, throughout the series government authorities exhibit behavior ranging from unhelpful to incompetent to cruel. There are, however, some notable differences. In *Stranger Things* we see greater redemption for our struggling local police official, Sheriff Hopper, and unlike *E.T. the Extra-Terrestrial*, many of the government officials have a face. In some cases they have a friendly face, like Dr. Owens in Season Two.

At the start of the series we see Hopper, obviously hung over, arrive late at the station. When his administrative assistant tells him Will is missing, he nonchalantly replies, "Hmmmm, I am going to get on that. Just give me a minute" ("Chapter One: The Vanishing of Will Byers"). After being pressed, he simply responds, "Mornings are for coffee and contemplation" ("Chapter One: The Vanishing of Will Byers"). Throughout the first few episodes of the series, Joyce has to beg Hopper to take her son's disappearance seriously. While Hopper is a less-than-ideal authority figure, as noted in chapter 2, we must also acknowledge that he is the product of institutional failures as well. His indifference stems from his own trauma, not necessarily incompetence or even disbelief. Also as mentioned in chapter 2, we find out his daughter died of cancer, and his marriage did not survive her death. At the start of Season One, it is clear he is suffering, barely coping with the trauma. In Season Three the mayor references this trauma as a way to hurt Hopper, which suggests Hopper is still reeling. These moments humanize Hopper and help the audience feel sympathy toward him. On the other hand, the police officers in the 1980s dataset have limited backstories, making it difficult for audiences, and other characters, to empathize with them.

Unlike the police officials in the 1980s dataset, Hopper eventually finds redemption by allying with the geeky kids and traumatized adults in their fight against the larger authority, the United States government (Seasons One and Two) and Russian agents (Season Three). There is a clear disconnect and distrust between Hopper and his immediate—both literal and figurative—superiors. Like the Gen Xers in the 1980s dataset, Hopper is also skeptical whether or not law enforcement agencies will be helpful when they are needed most. In Season Three, when Joyce suggests he run a check on a license plate to find out who brutally attacked him, he states, "I think you have to lower your expectations, but I mean this is a state government agency" ("Chapter Four: The Sauna Test"). He recognizes the agency's flaws and what it means to be a cog in a large, often ineffectual system.

Hopper's greatest moment of redemption is in Season Two, when he secures a birth certificate for Eleven. He is also offered a very humanizing moment at the end of Season Three via a speech he wrote for, but did not give to, Eleven. He writes: "Keep on growing up, kid. Don't let me stop you. Make mistakes, learn from 'em, and when life hurts you—because it will—remember the hurt. The hurt is good. It means you're out of that cave" ("Chapter Eight: The Battle of Starcourt"). Through this letter, he shares just how much Eleven means to him—how, in many ways, he not only saved her, they saved each other. It is a touching moment, and one that allows the audience to see a much softer side of Hopper.

The way in which the series represents government agents is also different. In Season One of *Stranger Things*, the behavior by government officials is more cruel than incompetent, similar to what we see in *E.T. the Extra-Terrestrial*. Eleven escapes from government custody, where she has been subject to horrific experiments studying her telekinetic powers. The *New York Daily News* notes how Eleven's experience echoes conspiracy

theories surrounding the Montauk Project, in which some
believe "children with psychic sensitivity were both sought
out and kidnapped—not unlike Eleven—with the hopes of
enhancing their latent abilities, perhaps for use in psychologi-
cal warfare" (Schladebeck). Her name—Eleven—is tattooed on
her, a dehumanizing symbol, echoing unthinkable acts of World
War II. In episode two of the series, Eleven's flashbacks show her
isolated in a small dark room as she calls for Papa, who really is
the scientist who kidnapped her at birth. Throughout the first
season, we see many faceless government officials chase Eleven,
offering perhaps the most overt example of government venality.

Conversely, in Season Two, the children encounter one helpful government official. He isn't, however, at first trustworthy.
Near the end of the second season, as the shadow monster
begins to overtake Will, Dr. Owens downplays the government's incompetence by noting that science, over the years,
has made abundant mistakes. To this end, Nancy points out
that "science" killed Barb. Dr. Owens repeats that, yes, Barb's
death was an abundant mistake. Throughout this exchange
with Nancy and Jonathan, Dr. Owens is very dismissive, but
at the same time, he also tries to reassure the teenagers that
the persons responsible for those horrific mistakes are no longer making decisions. While perhaps mildly comforting, this
excuse likely sounds familiar to viewers. It is offered regularly by
politicians, and has been heard by Gen Xers throughout their
lifetime. Like in the "Morning in America" commercial, politicians are quick to state how much better their administrations
will do than previous administrations. It is not uncommon to
hear politicians say that while previous administrations made
numerous mistakes, their administrations will not. Like Dr.
Owens, these politicians argue they are only there "to make
things better" ("Chapter Four: Will the Wise").

At this point *Stranger Things* diverges *significantly* from the 1980s dataset. Dr. Owens, in a rare feat of transparency, shows them all the portal to the Upside Down. Like the scientist that helps Elliot in *E.T. the Extra-Terrestrial*, we get the feeling Dr. Owens's allegiance is to science, closing the portal to the Upside Down, and saving Will. Unlike the nameless government official within the dataset, Dr. Owens not only has a name, he also gets more screen time to demonstrate his commitment to the children. Additionally, the Duffer brothers cast well-known 1980s actor Paul Reiser in the role; given Reiser's amount of screen time in Season Two as well as his fame outside of *Stranger Things*, he is far from faceless. Furthermore, despite being partially responsible for the events unfolding, Dr. Owens urges his team to consider alternative solutions to the problem, as burning the Upside Down might kill Will. If at all possible, he wants to save him. It is at this moment we get a sense that he actually cares—at least to some degree.

While he often has to be coaxed to do the right thing, Dr. Owens ultimately does and, like Hopper, is offered redemption. Later in the series, Dr. Owens further helps the group by obtaining a birth certificate for Eleven with the name "Jane Hopper" on it. This allows Eleven to live a more normal life. She can now be seen out in public and enroll in school (although the series never explains how Hopper adopted her). In Season Three, Joyce and Hopper call Dr. Owens when they realize they might need back up to stop the Russians from opening the portal to the Upside Down. Despite jokes about the timeliness of the government's response and Dr. Owens's assistance, Joyce and Hopper believe Dr. Owens is their best ally, their best shot at beating the Russians. Here *Stranger Things* questions blind loyalty to authority and the effectiveness of government institutions, similar to the 1980s dataset; however, unlike the

1980s dataset, it also recognizes that, at least at an individual level, there can be good people within each institution. Dr. Owens's helpful behavior by no means mitigates what happened to Eleven in Season One, or Will in Season Two, or the town and Hopper in Season Three, but it does offer some penance for the government's ghastly behavior.

Despite encountering helpful individuals, in *Stranger Things* (and the 1980s dataset), there is a sense that the government as a whole—with all its money, resources, and technology—are unable to help (even if willing). Once again, Gen Xers (like Nancy in *Nightmare on Elm Street*) must take matters into their own hands. To help Will in Season One, for example, it is left up to common citizens, with pieces of paper and a few crayons, to make sense of the situation—and make sense of it they do. In other instances in *Stranger Things*, the lack of assistance comes in the form of encouraging citizens to engage in vigilante justice (much like in *Nightmare on Elm Street*), as Kali and the other teens track down and punish the adults that hurt them. She tells Eleven, "We simply make them pay for their crimes" ("Chapter Seven: The Lost Sister"). This approach, however, has consequences for both Nancy and Kali: Nancy is forced to watch her friends die one by one until she is able to stop Freddy; Kali is forced to live a life on the run because she is wanted for her crimes. We see significant collateral damage when political and legal systems are eroded, including individuals turning to vigilante justice.

Take on Me: Another Layer of Harm

It is worth nothing that not all government intervention is *overtly* harmful. Some is more surreptitiously harmful. This type of harm, relatively absent from the 1980s dataset, is featured in *Stranger Things*. For example, in Season One, the fact that Will is the one who goes missing is, as others have noted, reflective of the fact that single mothers are often besieged by governmental policy, ultimately aiding in the negative public perception of them. As Coleman and Ganong note, even in 2010, "the public tends to associate single parenthood with laziness and an unwillingness to work." As mentioned previously, Joyce's single mother status is the reason she is not home to greet Will the night he goes missing, and her single mother status, as noted above, likely affects how she is treated when she reports Will missing. This theme is also explored via Eleven, as she is the child of a single mother being held for government experiments. Will and Eleven are, in fact, easy targets because they are products of single-family homes. Both situations were unlikely to occur in two-parent households. Because society often views single mothers as unstable and easily manipulated, their children are deemed expendable. The next section explores what happens to all children when there are broad institutional failures.

Systems Failure

Both *Back to the Future I* and *Back to the Future II* explore the effects on society of broad institutional failures, including the government itself. In these movies, Zemeckis contrasts two time periods, sending a warning to viewers: This is where the United States is headed, and it is not a pleasant place to live. It should be no surprise this message was echoed by Reagan in his 1984 reelection campaign, given his noted love of *Back to the Future*. As noted at the beginning of the chapter, the most famous commercial from the campaign "featured white Americans in white American small towns doing things that seemed out of the 1950s and asked, 'Why would we ever want to return to where we were less than four short years ago?'" (Smokler).

For example, in the first movie, the contrast between 1955 and 1985 is jarring and reflects the eroding of government services. The park is full of litter, suggesting a lack of civic funds or infrastructure. There is a homeless guy sitting on a bench in a small town, a sight generally associated with urban settings, suggesting a failure of the economy. Finally, there is a terrorism. In *Back to the Future II*, in future time, there is total institutional collapse. The school is gone, and law enforcement is corrupt, only there to serve Biff, who proudly proclaims, "I own the police" (*Back to the Future II*). We see what happens when police are bought and paid for, as it erodes not only the justice and penal systems but also other institutions as well. This is not to say the past is without its faults, and as noted earlier, *Back to the Future II* critiques this overly romanticized version of it.

Through the success of Biff's Pleasure Paradise, Biff, the epitome of an untrustworthy, selfish politician, is able to buy the community and, as part of the community, the police. When the viewer first gets a glimpse into this world, they hear and see a video describing Biff's entrepreneurial exploits playing on a loop for all Hill Valley citizens. At the end of the video, the video cuts to Biff saying, "God Bless America." The video shows him marrying Marty's mom; Biff says, "Third time's a charm." Since the 2016 election, there has been some discussion as to whether or not we have reached this point in our own history: bought and paid for politicians using fear and faux patriotism as well as religion to garner support from citizens. What has happened during the years between the 1980s dataset and *Stranger Things*—and how these events impacted the series—is discussed in more detail in the next chapter.

(You Gotta) Fight for Your Right (to Party): Learning When to Trust

Throughout the 1980s dataset and *Stranger Things*, we see a contrast in how different generations treat authority and are treated by authority. One poignant moment in *Stranger Things* is a scene between Karen and Ted in which Karen is restless waiting for the police to find her son and his friends. She indicates to her husband, Ted, that they should be out looking for them, urging him to act. In response, Ted provides the most appropriate late–Silent Generation/early–Baby Boomer comment: "Honey, we have to trust them, OK? This is our government. They're on our side" ("Chapter Seven: The Bathtub"). This is a stark contrast to the children who question authority, skeptical as to whether the government can help them, in order to save their friend Will. Throughout our time spent with the children of Hawkins, we come to see a need for balance; at times it is appropriate to trust, and at other times it is appropriate not to. Ted's response and the children's response are suitable, however, given how each generation is treated. The differences make sense given how each generation is viewed and treated by society. As mentioned previously, Gen Xers are often seen as suspect.

In Season One, Hopper becomes involved in the investigation and plays a crucial role in finding Will. Additionally, in Season Two, the children eventually team with Dr. Owens to save Will from the shadow monster. As noted in this chapter, this is a stark contrast to the 1980s dataset. In the dataset, there are no moments of redemption for officials working for the federal government. The absence is noteworthy and striking. Within the 1980s dataset, there is not ONE helpful police officer. The closest representation to a helpful or humane government official is the scientist in *E.T.*, and even in that scene the viewer is under the impression that the scientist is not so much an agent of the government as an academic. Rather, as noted previously, his allegiance is to science.

Despite these moments of redemption offered to individuals in *Stranger Things*, there is still a level of skepticism present. The series suggests that it is important to be wary of authority figures because it is very likely they will let everyday citizens down. In fact, depending on how one reads the series, in some ways the government does win—and wins at the expense of the children (Gen Xers) in the series. At the end of Season One, for example, Will is found, when Eleven seemingly defeats the monster; she, however, falls victim to the self-sacrificing trope. This trope plays out through each of the seasons. While Will is returned, the drastic effects of their experiments are explored in Season Two, and he is further tormented by this parallel world and the monster that resides within. In Season Three, Eleven loses her powers, and Hopper is missing.

As noted in the introduction, Reagan played into the fears of everyday Americans during his 1984 campaign, using nostalgia for the "wholesome" 1950s to garner additional votes. But, as we saw in *Stand by Me*, this time period was also fraught with problems, most notably familial strife under the picture-perfect surface. As 2021 viewers tune in to the fourth season of *Stranger Things*, they should ask: are the Duffer brothers playing on these very same fears? The country is in the midst of another great divide, including racial and political turmoil and ongoing and continued threats to the environment. In some ways, *Stranger Things* looks to a "simpler" time when it was a little clearer who and what to trust. As noted in the beginning of this chapter, this is something that has always been appealing to Gen Xers. If one was to describe Gen X's political agenda, it would be to "make things simple."

In the next chapter, I examine what has happened to Gen X between the 1980s dataset and *Stranger Things*. While the Duffer brothers are quick to expose the paradoxical nature of the 1980s, and the cynicism that festered, they also offer some hope. In the end, Hopper is helpful, and Dr. Owens wants to save Will. Despite the hopeful cynicism the series offers, it represents a time that is often referred to as more innocent (riding bikes around the neighborhood unsupervised, for example). This reason for these deviations between the 1980s dataset and *Stranger Things* is perhaps best explained by events that have taken place since 1989. At middle age, while Gen X remains cynical, they also have helped support, and in some cases redefine and revise, some of the very institutions they held suspect in their youth. Chapter 5 explores their journey.

— 5 —
Can't Knock the Hustle
Gen X as Adults

At the time of this publication, the youngest Gen Xers are approaching middle age. They have full-time jobs and families. They volunteer in their communities and participate in politics. Their work, however, is often unseen, as Gen Xers typically contribute to their communities through small, quiet gestures as opposed to large, loud ones (Gordinier, 163). Their behind-the-scenes work and lack of self-promotion is perhaps one reason why Gen Xers are unable to shake some of the unfavorable characteristics used to describe them in their youth: apathetic, individualistic, and uncommitted (Watson, xii). As the "slacker" insignia endures, Gen X continues to be dismissed by mainstream society; consumer markets and politicians continue to focus on those born before and after Gen X (Watson, xii). Except for a brief period of time in the 1990s, Gen Xers have spent most of their lifetime overlooked by those with political, business, social, and educational affluence.

As noted by Alex Williams, journalist for the *New York Times*, Gen X's cultural moment was short-lived. Eventually, and somewhat ironically, Gen Xers did become more widely known; they became known for being a small, forgettable blip among a series of much larger ones. This ultimately led to additional labels being used to describe them. Gen Xers have been called the forgotten generation and, affectionately, the forgotten middle child. The latter name is in reference to being sandwiched between two much larger, and thus more influential, generations: Baby Boomers and Millennials (Williams). These labels have resonated with Gen Xers, many using the descriptors to describe themselves and their peers, seeing "forgotten" as a badge of honor. Many Gen Xers have been delighted to remain on the fringes of society, an area occupied in their youth.

Rather fittingly, in January 2019, CBSN, CBS's 24/7 digital streaming news service, forgot to include Gen X on a graphic that listed generations and birth years for a story about Millennials (Mazza). The graphic immediately went viral. Gen Xers from around the United States commented on their omission, and the responses, as noted by many, clearly reflected the values and attitudes of Gen X. For instance, in response to the graphic, Gen X comedian Patton Oswalt adeptly tweeted, "As a member of Gen X, I am 100% cool with being left out of this mess" (@pattonoswalt). Other Gen Xers were happy to once again be forgotten, delighted to remain uninvolved in the social, political, and economic turmoil plaguing the United States. One Twitter user wrote, citing a skit from the late night comedy show *Saturday Night Live*, "I'm #GenX. I just sit on the sidelines and watch the world burn. -#keenanthompson @ nbcsnl" (Davis). Nearly two decades after the grunge movement and Gen X's cultural blip ended, this story highlights how Gen X continues to be forgotten. As seen in numerous tweets in the aftermath of their CBSN omission, it appears that Gen X has warmly embraced, if not relished in, this status.

In this chapter, I explore what has happened to Gen X since the 1980s dataset was released. I discuss why stereotypes persist despite Gen X serving as productive members of society for decades, often working directly against the negative stereotypes assigned to them in their youth. Throughout this chapter, I examine the ways in which *Stranger Things* diverges from the 1980s dataset and how these differences can be explained based in part on the experiences of forgotten, and often stereotyped, middle-aged Gen Xers. Just as the experiences of their youth influenced and were reflected in the 1980s dataset, Gen X's middle-age experiences are also reflected in, and influenced by, current popular culture, including *Stranger Things*. My focus remains on Gen X's interactions with three key institutions: the economy, their family, and the government. Throughout my analysis, I direct my attention toward three large social media movements: Occupy Wall Street, Me Too, and Black Lives Matter. I believe these movements—watershed cultural moments in our country—have shaped Gen X's evolving attitudes toward important issues facing each of the above institutions: income disparity, gender equity and familial roles, and law and order.

First, I examine how adult Gen Xers continue to navigate a very volatile economy, including living through several recessions, especially the Great Recession of 2008. These recessions plagued Gen X's upward mobility, increased income disparity, and culminated in 2011's Occupy Wall Street Movement, a movement which sought to highlight income inequality in the country. I examine how this movement was perceived by Gen Xers. Additionally, I examine how Gen Xers, despite financial difficulties, have prioritized family and worked tirelessly to grow and nurture their communities as well as to rebuild and expand their family units. In my analysis, it is clear these two

institutions intersect. Many of the familial decisions made by
Gen Xers are, at least in part, informed by the economic health
of the country and consequently of their families.

For example, the Great Recession both strengthened Gen
X's commitment to family while deepening their cynicism
toward the economy. Despite these hardships, however, the
recession did not necessarily prevent Gen Xers from turning to
an old friend: conspicuous consumption. For many Gen Xers,
this was the first time in their lives they had some disposable
income (Fry). Yet, despite having disposable income, Gen Xers
tend to favor experience over goods, suggesting, once again,
they value time/experiences with their family. I document how
these attitudes toward economics and familial experiences have
influenced plotlines in *Stranger Things*, including the addition
of more favorable representations of nontraditional families.
Nonetheless, despite these nontraditional representations, the
series suggests that while nuclear families are often tarnished
(and often reflected as thus in 1980s popular culture), nontraditional families also have significant interpersonal and financial
problems. *Stranger Things* demonstrates that sometimes the
healthiest familial relationships are not defined by the number
of parents living in one house, but rather by other factors. This
is evident in how Gen X has chosen to live their lives.

Additionally, I examine how *Stranger Things* explores the
concept of intersectionality, a concept absent from the 1980s
dataset. Intersectionality, or the intersection of identity mak-
ers, came to light during the third wave feminist movement in
the mid-1990s, a movement led by Gen Xers. Intersectionality
highlights how markers (gender, race, socioeconomic class, etc.)
intersect to shape people's experiences. Intersectionality was
again brought into light with the rise of the Me Too Movement
beginning in 2017, a movement aimed at exposing gender

inequality, harassment, and assault. Moira Donegan, writer for the *Guardian*, explains how intersectionality has affected the Me Too Movement. She believes that intersectionality has given "#MeToo a more expansive understanding of sexual harassment and assault. The gesture of saying 'me too' implies solidarity with all women who have had these experiences, but the form the movement has taken has also allowed for it to be a specific, personal declaration, and for those testimonies to come from women with different stories and in different circumstances" (Donegan). Given this rather prominent cultural movement, it makes sense that Season Three of *Stranger Things*, which aired in 2019, would focus more on gender and agency. In my analysis, I explore how *Stranger Things* diverges from the 1980s dataset to highlight issues brought forth by the Me Too Movement as well as intersectionality in general.

Finally, I analyze Gen X's current relationship with authority, specifically the continued fragile relationships between Gen Xers and politicians and Gen Xers and law enforcement. Part of my focus examines Gen Xers of color and how their relationship with law enforcement is reflected in and influenced by the Black Lives Matter movement, a movement highlighting violence against black people and systemic racism within law enforcement and the justice system. This movement, and the tension that it highlights, remains absent from *Stranger Things*. While *Stranger Things* fails to address the concerns raised by the Black Lives Matters Movement, it does accurately reflect Gen Xers' inclusivity and desire to include marginalized individuals in popular culture.

Additionally, while many Gen Xers remain skeptical of government officials at both the national and local levels, Gen Xers recognize the individual work of their peers in these types of positions and use these positions to advance their own perspectives. Since reaching adulthood, Gen Xers have worked government jobs and held political office. As such, it makes sense that Gen Xers would support *some* of these individuals within these institutions, given the value they place on peer relationships. This is ultimately reflected in *Stranger Things*. For example, as I note in chapter 4, *Stranger Things* provides moments of redemption for certain government agents. This slight shift in perspective is plausible given Gen Xers' current relationship with authority, as many Gen Xers work in these positions or profit from them. Despite these contradictions and paradoxes, my analysis shows how Gen X continues to foster a cynicism toward these institutions. I begin by taking a deeper look at Gen X's continued economic struggles and speculate as to how these struggles are reflected in *Stranger Things*.

Under the Bridge: The Great Recession and Gen X

Throughout modern history, it has been expected that each generation would fare better financially than the previous one; it was expected that children would find greater financial prosperity than their parents. As Gen Xers approached adulthood, however, this was no longer the case. In addition to fighting limited economic mobility, Gen X was the first generation that faced postsecondary education as a necessity for economic success. Despite this necessity, however, a degree did not *guarantee* financial success and a comfortable lifestyle for coming-of-age Gen Xers, leaving some with a degree but struggling to pay their student loans and household bills. Because of these factors, there was a growing cynicism festering throughout Gen X; many speculated that the American Dream was no longer achievable. Data support this concern, as economic mobility has been relatively stagnant for Gen Xers throughout their life. According to Erin Currier of the Pew Charitable Trusts:

> About 40 percent of those raised by low-income parents remain low-income themselves, and about 40 percent of those raised by high-income parents end up high income. For Gen X, this stickiness at the bottom is even more pronounced than for other generations: Half of Gen Xers raised at the bottom remain stuck there themselves, and nearly three-quarters never reach the middle. Similarly, 40 percent of those raised at the top remain there as adults, and more than two-thirds never fall to the middle. In fact, 7 in 10 Gen Xers at the top rung of the income ladder in their 30s were raised by parents who were also above the middle in their 30s.

Throughout adulthood, Gen Xers have faced several challenges: limited upward mobility (as noted above), financial troubles, and economic uncertainty. One of the primary reasons for their limited economic mobility was a series of economic recessions throughout their lifetime (early 1980s, early 1990s, 2001, and 2008). During the global economic downturn called the Great Recession (2008), Gen Xers lost a substantial amount of money and assets, more than other generations. In 2008, according to Richard Fry, Pew Research Center analyst, "The median net worth of Gen X households had declined 38% from 2007 ($63,400) to 2010 ($39,200), while the typical wealth loss for Boomer and Silent households was not as steep (26% and 14%, respectively)." While the Great Recession also harmed Millennials, they were less affected by it because they had less to lose, given their age. Despite Millennials being less affected by the recession, they were quick to respond, playing a large role in a social media movement that sought to highlight the financial troubles of many Americans.

The Occupy Wall Street Movement

In 2011, primarily in response to the limited economic opportunities for the majority of Americans, the Occupy Wall Street (OWS) movement was formed. While the movement did not adhere to any specific principles or put forth specific demands, it largely focused on income equality and wealth distribution, seeking to expose how America's largest companies continued to see record-breaking profits while many of their workers continued to struggle to pay for basic necessities. In February 2011, Canadian anti-consumerist magazine *Adbusters* encouraged people to fight back against these large corporations that sought to maximize profits at the expense of workers. In the issue's editorial, staff writer Kono Matsu stated, "Blatant corruption rules at the heart of American democracy. And with corporations now treated as people, big business money dictates who is elected to Congress and what laws they shall pass. America has devolved into a corporate state ruled by and for the mega-corps" (Da Silva). And with that issue of *Adbusters* and Matsu's editorial, the OWS began.

The movement's leaderless, decentralized model made use of social media to spread its message nationwide. Citizens from across the United States tweeted in support of the movement, sharing their own personal financial struggles as evidence. Additionally, Facebook pages for similar movements, tied to specific cities, were formed (Ngak), and on September 17, 2011, more than a thousand protestors occupied New York City's Zuccotti Park, a public park near Wall

Street, claiming they were the "99 percent," referring to income and wealth inequality (Da Silva).

Because it was decentralized, the OWS movement was also leaderless, although Millennial/Xennial Micah White, former editor of *AdBusters*, is often cited as the architect of the concept. Gen Xers, who struggled with income inequality for years, had mixed feelings toward the movement. Some supported it, noting the widening income gap and citing their own personal struggles; others, however, believed that Millennials, a large portion of those supporting the movement, wanted too much for free ("Occupy Wall Street Movement"). Gen Xers who were against the movement generally believed that if they were able to persevere despite little to no help, so could those protesting. In that regard, Reagan's vision of the American Dream—including the "pull yourself up by your bootstraps" narrative—was very much alive. Even though many Gen Xers were skeptical whether the American Dream existed, many supported the overall idea behind it. Perhaps one reason for the latter perspective was that despite the devastating blow to Gen X's financial stability in 2008, many Gen Xers bounced back from the Great Recession due to home equity and having a good number of working years left (Fry). Despite this, more so than Baby Boomers and Millennials, Gen Xers continue to be pessimistic as to whether or not they will have enough money to retire (Taylor and Gao). This could be due to the fact that even when the national economy is healthy, Gen Xers have struggled with upward mobility within their own industries, leading to greater pessimism in regard to retirement and cynicism toward work in general.

For example, it has been widely noted that Gen Xers are often the most overlooked for promotion. In a 2018 article for CNBC, Stephanie Neal and Richard Wellins write: "Gen X leaders on average had only 1.2 promotions in the past 5 years, significantly lower than their younger millennial counterparts (1.6 promotions) and more senior baby boomers (1.4 promotions) during the same period of time." This could be one reason as to why they are less likely to be loyal to one company. More so than other generations, Gen X is more likely to switch jobs, pursuing "greener financial pastures and more conducive work environments" (Watson, xiv). Some might assume that the generation labeled as slackers are not being promoted because of their work ethic; this, however, is not necessarily the case. There are several reasons offered for Gen X's lack of promotions, including their desire to prioritize family over work. Additionally, it has been noted that Gen X tends to be more humble, which causes them to go unnoticed by supervisors.

Gordinier argues that one of the primary reasons Gen X is overlooked for promotions is because of how Gen X was raised. Citing a movie often watched by coming-of-age Gen Xers, *Willy Wonka and the Chocolate Factory*, Gordinier notes that Gen X learned most of their life lessons from the movie, including the importance of being humble. Specifically, Gen Xers were taught that "it's wrong to sell out, it's wrong to want to be the center of attention, it's wrong to be too grasping and transparent in your ambitions" (Gordinier, 77). While clearly not favored in the chocolate factory, these qualities tend to be favored in the workforce. On many occasions, Gen Xers do not self-advocate and are thus often overlooked for management positions, causing decreased economic mobility. The next section examines how the OWS movement, Gen Xers' continued economic strife, and their consequent economic cynicism are reflected in *Stranger Things*.

Economic Uncertainty and the Upside Down

The fact that Gen Xers have experienced a lifetime of economic downturns and financial hardships may be one reason why *Stranger Things* does not deviate drastically from the 1980s dataset in regard to how our economic system is represented. If anything, the income gap has widened since the release of the movies, making the issue even more prevalent in current popular culture. This is perhaps why there is such a contrast between the haves and the have-nots in the series. Season One and Season Two highlight how the gap has created a gulf in suburbia, via the juxtaposition of the Byers and Wheeler families. These representations serve as a way to draw attention to the vast income inequality in the United States. In Season Three, however, there is a much broader critique of the economic system as a whole, namely the effects of unchecked capitalism: the rich getting richer and the poor getting poorer as well as small mom-and-pop stores going out of business because they are unable to compete with large corporations. This ultimately echoes some of the concerns raised by the OWS movement. The series suggests that capitalism, touted as an ideal tenet of the United States, may also be the country's weakness when left unregulated. The series demonstrates how unbridled capitalism can be harmful to many, including families. As such, it would be remiss not to discuss how representations of the widening income gap intersect with family, because at its core *Stranger Things* is about family.

Family Affair: The Growing Nuclear Family

The previous section mentioned ways in which *Stranger Things* reflects the widening income gap. In this instance, the representation of family is also intertwined with economic critique. In chapter 3 I discuss how the widening income gap was implicitly addressed in the series, namely through representations of the haves (Wheeler family) and have-nots (Byers family). Couching economic critique within familial representation is appropriate, however, given how Gen X views family: first, in whatever form it takes, family is highly valued; and second, the economy has all but *required* a redefining of the family unit. As Watson notes, many Gen Xers have "redefined the meaning of family" because of economic conditions and their upbringing (xii).

Since entering adulthood, Gen Xers sought to avoid making the same mistakes made by their parents, costly mistakes such as divorce. For example, a 2015 study revealed that Gen Xers have the highest rates of marriage and partnering (Vernon). When they were children, their parents emphasized the positive aspects of divorce; despite this, survey data suggests that only one-fifth of Gen X children of divorce were actually happier when their parents split (Howe and Strauss, *13th Gen*, 60). Upon entering adulthood, Gen Xers sought to change this and began "to construct the strong families that they missed in childhood" (Howe and Strauss, "The Next 20 Years," 45). According to *Salon* writer Sara Scribner, "Many Xers seem nostalgic for the serene '50s childhood that they never had and they have been pretty focused on creating a solid home life for their children, whether it's from re-creating the idyllic family-oriented tableaux depicted in an Ikea catalog or jarring their own preserves." We see glimpses of this perspective in *Ferris Buller's Day Off*, throughout which there is an ongoing discussion between Ferris and Sloan about marriage. At one point, Ferris looks at the camera and states, "I was serious when I said I would marry her" (*Ferris Bueller's Day Off*). Despite the will they/won't they throughout the entire movie, Sloan admits, "He's gonna marry me" (*Ferris Bueller's Day Off*). Marriage, for these Gen Xers, was seen as a desirable institution.

For adult Gen Xers, "starting and maintaining a stable family can be a unique source of pride—the pride you get for achieving something your parents did not" (Howe and Strauss, *Millennials Rising*, 56). Rather than using their cynicism to tear apart the institutions of marriage and family, they worked to redefine and restore the integrity of them. Acknowledging that there are different fulfilling ways to live, Gen X worked to define a satisfying lifestyle, despite social and economic factors.

According to the Pew Research Center, "A record 57 million Americans, or 18.1% of the population of the United States, lived in multi-generational family households in 2012, double the number who lived in such households in 1980" (Fry and Passel). Gen Xers also sought to embrace extended-family living situations, including allowing, even encouraging, their adult children to live at home. Anna Sofia Martin, contributor to website Next Avenue, notes: "Kids used to flee the nest, but now they're also coming back home—in droves—to their Gen X parents. Adults in their 20s and 30s are crashing with their parents at record or near-record levels. Instead of downsizing as they age, some Gen X'ers are *upsizing* to accommodate their extended families." Two aspects are said to be the driving force behind this shift in thinking: strong family values and economic necessity. Despite early skepticism toward nuclear families living the "perfect" life in suburbia, Gen X is also known to be remarkably loyal to family members and friends.

Furthermore, unlike many of their parents, Gen Xers strive for work-life balance. It has been widely noted that Gen Xers prefer jobs that offer flexible scheduling to take care of family obligations; they expect employers to accommodate their work/family issues (Beutell and Wittig-Berman, 519). Boomers, by contrast, have been found to value work that can be accomplished over working regularly scheduled business hours (Rodriquez, Green, and Ree). As soon as Gen Xers believe their values are not compatible with an organization, they are prepared to leave; their loyalty, it seems, is to their skills rather than to their employers. We see this reflected in *Stranger Things*, as the series explores what happens when one does not prioritize family (whether willingly in the case of Karen or unwillingly in the case of Joyce).

It is said that, because children in the 1980s were often alone, Gen X learned to be more independent than previous generations. In addition, Gen Xers also look for community and family outside of previous definitions: "because Gen Xers, speaking in the most general terms, aren't tethered to family and other institutions in the ways that their predecessors were, they create a comforting cocoon of artifice" (Hanson, 43). Even for Gen Xers from two-parent households, like Mike and Nancy, family was expanded to encompass friends and community groups.

For example, friends band together to save the family house in *The Goonies*. Friends, not family, encourage Chris in *Stand by Me* to overcome trouble at home and eventually go off to college. In two separate scenes in *Stand by Me*, we see the boys open up to one another to the point of tears. At one point, Chris tells Gordie he is going to be a great writer and reassures him that his dad "doesn't hate you; he just doesn't know you" (*Stand by Me*). *Stranger Things* continues this motif, highlighting the value Gen Xers place on friendships. In all three seasons, we see friends became so close they are like family. In Season One friends search for Will when he is trapped in the Upside Down world. In Season Two friends help Eleven fight to shut the Upside Down portal. Finally, in Season Three, friends band together to fight the Russians and the mind flayer. The Season One tagline, "a friend is someone you'd do anything for..." reflects an unwavering commitment to peers ("Stranger Things").

As a result of continued income inequality and lack of upward mobility, although they are now in a different stage in life, Gen Xers still have many of the same fears they did as young adults, resulting in similar cynical feelings toward economic institutions and agents. Since uncertainty remains for Gen Xers, it makes sense that what was felt and reflected in 1980s popular culture would be reflected in *Stranger Things*. While the 1980s dataset (*The Goonies*, *The Breakfast Club*, and *Ferris Bueller's Day Off*) had more overt references to the economy, particularly in regard to conspicuous consumption, *Stranger Things* very prominently highlights the widening income gap and its effect on families, namely via the comparison of Joyce and Karen and to a lesser extent their children, Jonathan and Nancy. While the Joyce/Karen comparison serves as a vehicle to highlight economic disparity, it also serves to critique the patriarchal culture of the 1980s, a critique strikingly absent from the 1980s dataset. In the next section I explore how patriarchal culture is reflected and challenged in *Stranger Things*, including how it influences familial and peer relationships.

Miss Independent: The Women of *Stranger Things*

As I note in chapter 2, the Joyce/Karen binary highlights the widening income gap and suggests that single-parent house-holds can be just as nurturing as, if not more than, two-parent households. As one watches *Stranger Things*, it is clear that two parents do not automatically create a happy household with happy children, and that money, or lack thereof, can strain familial relationships. The effects of the widening income gap are also illuminated via the children of Joyce and Karen, Jonathan and Nancy. Showing the effects of this gap and the limited economic opportunities for some, however, is not the only purpose these binaries serve in the series. The Joyce/Karen and Jonathan/Nancy binaries also support two other points worth exploring, points highlighted by another key cultural movement: the Me Too movement.

The Me Too Movement

First and foremost, the Karen/Joyce binary underscores the varying degrees of gender inequality, in addition to critiquing heteronormative patriarchal culture, a culture that was notably toxic in the 1980s. Other plot points support this analysis, namely via other female characters and their search for agency in Season Three. Furthermore, the Jonathan/Nancy binary highlights intersectionality—the interconnected nature of social identity markers such as race, gender, class, sexuality, ability, etc. Nancy's experiences (what happens to her and how she is treated) are shaped not merely by her socioeconomic class; they are also shaped by her race and gender. As themes, challenging toxic patriarchal culture and exploring intersectionality are unique to *Stranger Things* as they, for the most part, remain unexplored within the 1980s dataset.

This makes sense, however. While the influence of the OWS movement on the series was already noted, the Me Too movement also influenced the series. On one hand, the OWS movement highlighted corporate influence on democracy and the widening income gap; on the other hand, the Me Too movement has spotlighted a different type of danger, the pervasiveness of sexual assault and toxic masculinity in our society. During fall 2017, a year and a half before the third season of *Stranger Things* was released, women across the country from a variety of sectors but particularly in the entertainment industry, shared their stories of workplace abuse and harassment via social media and other platforms. It was the start of the Me Too era.

Remarkably, the movement gained momentum, and some of the men accused were questioned and held accountable by the public, including actor Kevin Spacey, producer Harvey Weinstein, and comedian Louis CK (Donegan). In Seasons One and Two *Stranger Things* focused on the widening income gap, and while that continues to be addressed in Season Three, it is clearly no longer the primary focus. Airing in 2019, Season Three pivots, focusing on many of the aspects discussed in light of the Me Too movement, including gender equity and harassment in the workforce. More so than previous seasons, Season Three examines what it is like to be a woman in a patriarchal culture.

Intersectionality and Toxic Patriarchy

Of note, the comparison of Joyce and Karen in *Stranger Things* explores what it means to be a woman in the 1980s (and arguably today). While Seasons One and Two primarily focus on their socioeconomic class, Season Three focuses on their socioeconomic class *and* how it intersects with other identity markers, like gender. Gen X played a critical role in ushering in third wave feminism, bringing intersectionality to light. Helene Shugart goes so far to suggest that third-wave feminism is "a subculture of the larger rhetorical phenomenon of Generation X rather than a phase or contemporary incarnation of feminism" (134). It makes sense, then, that Joyce and Karen, as well as their children, are used to highlight this very concept. A focal point of third-wave feminism is how socially constructed identity markers produce social inequality, specifically how different identity markers intersect, such as gender and class, creating interconnected systems of inequality.

It is clear from the representation of these two women how gender and economic factors collide to both oppress and privilege. We see how Joyce's experience in Hawkins is vastly different from Karen's. Not only are their experiences different from one another because of their socioeconomic class, but also their experiences are different from other characters because of their gender. Despite this, the series fails to explore the ways in which economic power is intertwined with social and political power except, perhaps, how Joyce is treated by law enforcement and government agents. As a poor single mother, she is repeatedly dismissed by not only neighbors, but also law enforcement. While the differences in class are highlighted prominently throughout Seasons One and Two, mostly via aesthetics, in Season Three *Stranger Things* shifts its focus to gender when it explores sexual harassment in the workforce and plight of female agency.

Sexism in the Workforce

In a Season Three we see a more overt focus on gender and gender discrimination and inequality. For example, after Nancy and Jonathan are fired from their internships for pursuing a story when they were told not to do so, their conversation briefly highlights intersectionality, as Jonathan realizes he cannot truly understand Nancy's experiences in the newsroom. Fed up from being treated terribly by the all-male staff, Nancy proclaims, "You don't know what it's like" ("Chapter Four: The Sauna Test"). With that said, while Nancy is forced to cope with sexist comments daily and is greatly limited in what she is allowed to do at work, Jonathan also struggles.

Unlike Nancy, Jonathan is concerned about money and, to a lesser extent, how people will perceive him because of his socioeconomic class. Because of his lived experiences as a child from a financially strapped single-parent household, Jonathan immediately retorts to Nancy, "Neither do you" ("Chapter Four: The Sauna Test"). In this exchange, it is clear they are both oppressed in different ways. Ultimately, Jonathan apologizes to Nancy, as he comes to realize that, despite his own struggles, he is afforded certain privileges in the newsroom because of his gender. Unlike Nancy, his work is taken seriously, and he is viewed as an emerging photojournalist by the newspaper staff. Generally speaking, he is respected. On the other hand, Nancy is viewed as the office servant; throughout her work at the newspaper, her primary responsibility was taking coffee and lunch orders. Despite her repeated efforts to learn from the staff and engage in journalistic activity, she is never given the opportunity to showcase her investigative talents.

Nancy's struggles, however, do not make Jonathan's struggles any less valid. Nancy fails to acknowledge this even after Jonathan apologizes to her. Their exchange—what is said and what is not said—highlights the primary focus of this season: gender equality for women. Natalia Dyer, the actor who plays Nancy, told the *Hollywood Reporter* that she was happy to have a more complex storyline in Season Three, noting how her character's situation in the newsroom is "so relatable" because "people are obviously still feeling this so much" (McVey). In that regard, this storyline, despite being set in the 1980s, very much speaks to middle-aged Gen Xers living in the Me Too moment.

Living in a Patriarchal Culture

Stranger Things also examines and critiques the toxic nature of the patriarchal 1980s culture in more implicit ways. As noted above, throughout Season Three Nancy is forced to deal with sexism and harassment while completing her internship; however, this is not the only way *Stranger Things* addresses this issue.

Even in earlier seasons, on a more macro level, *Stranger Things* is a series that seeks to subvert gender norms. According to blogger and popular culture critic Cameron Rout, the Upside Down world is symbolic of the chauvinistic patriarchal culture of the 1980s. It is not by accident, Rout notes, that characters who are traditionally oppressed defeat the shadow monster in Season One:

> The power of the Upside Down is as powerful and insurmountable as patriarchal chauvinism in the early 1980s. The idea that a rag-tag crew of teenagers in various stages of adolescence could even imagine standing up to its horrors is just as unbelievable that suburban high schoolers dressed in studded denim could team up with the Tolkien-worshipping basement dorks and stand up to the powerful influence of patriarchal chauvinism in 1983. (Rout)

In *Stranger Things*, those who have been oppressed by patriarchal culture (nerdy boys, men with feminine traits, and girls in general) are more likely to have agency, defeating the shadow monster and mind flayer, monsters of a patriarchal culture. While this is a theme throughout the series, it is not until Season Three that the young girls in the series truly are given agency.

For example, in Season Three, Eleven and Max go shopping at the mall, and what ensues is a scene oozing with female empowerment. Despite the problematic nature of conspicuous consumption in the scene as noted in chapter 3, the montage documents the girls obtaining a level of agency previously unseen in *Stranger Things* and nearly every mall-themed film of the 1980s. The moment is not defined by—or because of—any boys in the series. According to Michelle Delgado, writer for *The Atlantic*: "Though *Stranger Things*' third season at times feels weighed down by its references to '80s works, scenes at Starcourt expand upon their source material. Instead of reinforcing the social order or requiring female characters to continuously react to men and boys, Starcourt becomes a place where friendships are forged, identity is discovered, and monsters are conquered." In part spawned by the Me Too movement, Season Three of *Stranger Things* pivoted in how it constructed its female characters. Female actors were given more robust storylines with a greater focus on their characters as individuals and not as romantic pursuits. For the first time in the series, female characters were able to "flex their agency" (Delgado). The next section explores the ways in which each primary female character does so in the series.

Providing Agency to Marginalized Groups

Ani Bundel, writer for NBC News, observes how female characters "are given more agency and screen time this season, pushing the story forward, demanding their space and fighting back against the assumptions of the men around them." Throughout Season Three, the Duffer brothers spend more time developing their female characters, namely Joyce, Eleven, and Nancy. Additionally, we also see three new female characters, Robin, Erica, and Suzie, all of whom are empowered in different ways. Each of these new characters plays a critical role in saving Hawkins from the Russians and the mind flayer. Robin works with Steve and helps penetrate the Russians' headquarters. Erica is a regular at the local ice cream parlor, and this is where she meets Robin and Steve, who recruit her, based on her size, to help infiltrate the Russian offices underneath Starcourt Mall. Robin and Steve quickly learn that Erica is much more than her pint-sized frame; she is incredibly smart.

Finally, Suzie is Dustin's girlfriend from camp. While we only see her for one scene in the final episode, she plays a critical role in stopping the multiple looming threats facing the town, and she does so by using her immense scientific knowledge.

While Erica, Robin, and Suzie serve as a breath of fresh air (all are smart and articulate), some characters from previous seasons fall flat, particularly Karen. As noted in chapter 2, while Joyce actively helps the children in both small (day-to-day moments) and large ways (fighting the shadow monster), Karen remains oblivious to what is happening in her own home and in the Upside Down world. If we believe that the Upside Down is a symbol of patriarchal chauvinism, as noted by Rout, this would suggest that Karen remains oblivious to its occurrence in the "real" world (Rout). This claim is generally supported by the way in which Karen acts throughout the series, as she subscribes to and generally supports traditional gender roles. In Season Three, however, there is one scene in which Karen has a heart-to-heart talk with Nancy, suggesting that she *does* see the sexism around her but is too tired to do anything about it. At this moment it feels as though as Karen is not so much accepting of her situation as she is defeated by it.

While it is easy to dismiss Karen, to view her as a lonely, disinterested housewife, this key moment in Season Three suggests that Karen is more complex than our initial assessment. At the very least, we must acknowledge that Karen is a product of the era in which she was raised, struggling to escape the patriarchal culture that both provides for her and stifles her. While audiences may dislike Karen for upholding dated gender role stereotypes and heteropatriarchal values, her responses—to Joyce, to Nancy, to Ted—reflect her own experiences and the time period in which the show was set.

On the other hand, throughout the series Joyce is given agency to challenge existing norms and defeat the monster that inhabits the Upside Down and threatens her son (Seasons One and Two) and the Russian agents that inhabit her town (Season Three). There is a possible reason for these differences. Unlike Karen, Joyce is forced to squarely face some of these inequalities. As the sole provider for her boys, she regularly confronts these challenges, whereas Karen has the luxury of feeling frustrated, but also looking the other way, comfortable in her lifestyle. As noted by Nancy in an earlier season, Karen's life was cushy prior to her getting married (she came from a well-to-do family) and is even cushier now.

Some critics have argued that Joyce, despite receiving a good amount of screen time, is not a strong female character because her storyline only revolves around her son (Dickson; Grimes). Others, however, have argued that *Stranger Things* (at least in Seasons One and Two) is really Joyce's story, a story about maternal grief (Groom). In Season Three, however, there is a noticeable change in Joyce's storyline. Despite the boys and men being given adequate screen time, there is no doubt who the story is about. The story is not focused on saving Will; it is focused on saving the town. Joyce, as well as the other female characters, are no longer defined by their relationship to Will. As noted by *Variety* columnist Caroline Framke, due to criticism of Seasons One and Two, the Duffer brothers decided to focus on developing female characters in Season Three: "Season 3, to its credit, does real work to undo the previous seasons' stumbles by having Max and Eleven bond, Nancy committed to investigative journalism, and Joyce stand up more to Hopper's steamrolling. But it's still Robin who ends up breaking free of the show's typical tropes and running away with the season" (Framke).

For example, while Eleven was always *powered*, she was not *empowered*; however, this changes as her storyline is developed in Season Three, moving beyond her relationships with Will, Mike, and Hopper. Throughout the season there is quite a bit of discussion about Eleven's independence. Mike, now her boyfriend, is concerned that if she uses her powers too much, it will hurt her. Max, Eleven's friend, disagrees, arguing that Eleven should decide what is best for Eleven. Ultimately, Max encourages Eleven to be Eleven—not Mike's Eleven or Hopper's Eleven. In a tense moment, Max proclaims to Mike: "She is not yours. She is her own person, fully capable of making her own decisions" ("Chapter Six: E Pluribus Unum"). During this heated exchange, a nearby Nancy, who also has been struggling with the men in her life trying to control her, agrees. Obviously frustrated, Mike questions the context in which Max is arguing for Eleven's independence, stating he only wants what is best for her. Mike later apologizes to Eleven, and Eleven assures him she will be okay. Eleven does eventually lose her powers, and at the end of Season Three she has yet to gain them back. While she sacrificed her powers for the group, in this season she did so by *her* choice.

As noted above, the other female characters that shine are Erica and Suzie. Rarely do we see depictions of smart and engaging female *children*. Specifically, as noted by Germain Lussier, Cheryl Eddy, Beth Elderkin, and Charles Pulliam-Moore, "the great thing about Erica's arc and her realization is that it explicitly recognizes the role she plays within *Stranger Things*' narrative, a space that little black girls like Erica have been largely missing from in genre pop culture for far too long." Additionally, despite being in only one episode, Dustin's cross-country girlfriend Suzie plays an important role in fighting the Russians. Unlike all the other self-proclaimed male "nerds" in the series, she is the one character that remembers Planck's constant, a physical constant that is the quantum of electromagnetic action. It is a critical piece of information, as it is needed to close the portal.

Finally, in Season Three there is the introduction of one, possibly two, queer characters. In one of the more moving moments of the season, Robin, Steve's coworker, tells Steve she is gay. While Robin is a gay character, she is not one dimensional; she is not defined by her sexuality. Without her, for example, Steve and Dustin would likely never have cracked the Russian code to infiltrate their headquarters (they wouldn't have), and it is unclear how successful they would have been outsmarting the Russians and fighting the mind flayer. In addition to Robin, there is also one scene in which it is implied that Will might be gay. While the boys are playing Dungeons & Dragons, Will becomes frustrated that his friends would rather spend time with their girlfriends. Irritated, Mike exclaims, "It's not your fault you don't like girls" ("Chapter Three: The Case of the Missing Lifeguard"). After the outburst, the look between Will and Mike suggests the gravity of the statement. This subtly suggests that Will not liking girls has less to do with trying to hold onto his childhood innocence than him not being attracted to girls.

Having one and possibly two gay characters is a far cry from Seasons One and Two, in which there were no gay characters and a host of derogatory references to queer individuals—not uncommon in 1980s film. The change in the series is most reflected in Steve; in many ways, the series growth is his growth. In Season One, we hear Steve call Jonathan a queer; in Season Three, however, he responds to Robin much differently. When she shares that she is gay, he responds not with crude comments but with acceptance. These changes are positive, reflecting the current culture—much of which is highlighted by the Me Too movement. In the next section, I examine how Gen X's relationship with authority has evolved over their lifetime and how this evolution has impacted *Stranger Things*. The next section explores another shift between the 1980s dataset and series—specifically, the representation of government officials and how Gen X views these officials in real life.

The Charade: Gen X's Evolving Relationship with the Law

Throughout their lifetime, Gen Xers have watched "the government, the banking industry, law firms, and corporations be damaged or destroyed by greed, neglect, or incompetence" (Watson, xiv). They have watched corruption unfold, impacting them, their friends, and their family members. As adults, scandals such as Enron, WorldCom, and Bernie Madoff are etched in Gen X's memory (Watson, xiv), causing middle-aged Gen Xers to remain leery of authority, the same authority they questioned in their youth. Despite their skepticism, however, many Gen Xers actively participate in civic life and politics and recognize individual efforts within these sectors. As noted by Halstead, regardless of their active engagement in national politics, a cynicism remains. He cites Gary Ruskin, a Xer who directs the Congressional Accountability Project: "'Republicans and Democrats have become one and the same—they are both corrupt at the core and behave like children who are more interested in fighting with each other than in getting anything accomplished'" (quoted in Halstead). This feeling is reflected in their political leanings; from a partisan standpoint, a large number of Gen Xers identify as independents (Watson, xiv). According to a poll conducted by the Pew Research Center, Gen Xers equally align between both political parties, at least during presidential elections, giving the independent label some weight. In the 2008 presidential election, 52 percent of Gen Xers voted for Barack Obama and 46 percent for John McCain (Watson, xv). In the 2018 midterm elections, 48 percent of Gen Xers identified as Democrats or lean Democratic, while 43 percent identified as Republicans or lean Republican ("The Generation Gap").

While it might surprise some that the generation that ushered in the anti-authority grunge movement supports prominent Republican officials, if one considers their upbringing it isn't too much of a surprise. According to Neil Howe, as Gen Xers came of age, America was embracing individualism, materialism, and capitalism. This led to middle-aged Gen Xers who were "very naturally libertarian, very pragmatic" (Ramanathan). Howe goes on to state that Gen X's politics are the perfect reflection of their childhood: "No one is going to help you. No handouts. It's up to you. Particularly first-wave Xers, they're just naturally Republican" (Ramanathan). As such, 45 percent of Gen Xers believe that the government is doing too much, compared to 34 percent of Millennials and 29 percent of Gen Zers (Parker, Graf, and Igielnik). The next section outlines how these political beliefs are reflected in *Stranger Things* and how it compares to the 1980s dataset.

Current Views on Government and *Stranger Things*

As noted in the previous section, Gen Xers are highly skeptical of the government, often perceived to be linked to familial troubles, and have been for the majority of their lives. This is, of course, reflected within the 1980s dataset and *Stranger Things*.

For example, the story of Willy in *The Goonies*, as told by Mikey, is highly romanticized. Mikey explains that Willy was running from the Spanish government. Despite the fact that Willy actually stole the treasure, it is clear there is sympathy for his plight. This is likely reflective of their observations, for Gen Xers were raised to be skeptical of authority, including the government.

This is also reflected in *Stranger Things*, particularly in Season Three. Season Three is the first to feature a local politician, and he has a good amount of screen time. Throughout, Mayor Kline tries to silence his constituents when they express displeasure in his leadership, and he all but forces Hopper to *literally* silence them by forcing the protesters to disband. This character reflects some of Gen X's youthful and midlife fears in regard to government and politics: politicians are either corrupt and self-serving (best-case scenario) or domestic terrorists (worse-case scenario). In *Stranger Things*, Mayor Kline is clearly in cahoots with the Russians; his primary motive, however, seems to be lining his own pockets, not disrupting national security, suggesting he is more the self-serving sort. In that regard, much like the representations of law enforcement officials in the 1980s dataset discussed extensively in chapter 4, Mayor Kline is clearly inept, as he doesn't fully understand the consequences of his actions. Near the end of the season, it is clear he has no idea how much trouble his deal with the Russians is causing.

Despite being skeptical of corruption at both a national and local level, and of utter ineptness by officials at all levels, adult Gen Xers continue to show up for their communities, much like the way Joyce and Hopper do in *Stranger Things*. According to a study conducted by the Center for Information and Research on Civic Learning and Engagement, as college students Gen Xers were more focused on "getting ahead as individuals, not developing personal philosophies or participating as citizens" (Kiesa et al.). When they did engage civically, it was in the way of "individual acts of service, not political organizing or engagement with large institutions" (Kiesa et al.). It is often noted how the children of late Baby Boomers and early Gen Xers (Gen Yers/Millennials) have more experience with engagement, believing they have an "obligation to work together with others on social issues" (Kiesa et al.). According to Volunteering and Civic Life in America data, however, this characterization is a little misleading. In 2015, 28.9 percent of Gen Xers reported volunteering ("Generation X") whereas 21.9 percent of Millennials reported volunteering ("Millennials"). After 2005 Millennials' participation decreased, after most had graduated from high school. This might suggest that some of this volunteer work was mandated—or at least highly encouraged—by their parents. It seems as though Gen Xers, rather quietly, are giving back; despite their cynicism, they are showing up for their communities.

Black Lives Matter in Hawkins, Indiana

In chapter 4 I note how both government officials and law enforcement are offered redeeming moments in *Stranger Things*. This choice humanizes not only the individual, but also the institution as a whole. I have also noted earlier in this chapter how the series is influenced by two large cultural movements, movements largely led on social media: Occupy Wall Street and the Me Too movement. The social media movement that is strikingly absent, however, is the Black Lives Matter movement, aimed at raising awareness of systemic racism, namely toward black individuals.

Some scholars have noted how *Stranger Things* dances around the topic of racial inequality. For example, Aaron

Giovannone argues that Kali and her group of outcasts are reminiscent of the Rainbow Coalition, a coalition started in 1968 by Fred Hampton, an activist in the Black Panther Party; this "class-based coalition was a political innovation considered especially dangerous by law enforcement." He goes on to note how *Stranger Things* seems to support rainbow coalition politics (see: numerous rainbows throughout Season Two), but because of how law enforcement is represented throughout the series, it is a problematic endorsement as it is void of any class or racial critique (Giovannone).

In Season Two law enforcement is always shown as making the "right" decision. For example, Kali's gang always shoots first, and then police respond. Giovannone argues this does not reflect Hampton's own plight, as he was shot and killed by police, or the troubled modern-day relationships between people of color and law enforcement. During one scene Kali exclaims to Eleven, "Let me guess. Your police man tries to stop you from using your gifts" ("Chapter Seven: The Lost Sister"). Eleven, while agreeing with Kali, chooses to side with Hopper, returning to Indiana and consenting to being adopted by him. Giovannone argues this action ultimately reinforces and validates law enforcement behavior. He argues this representation is dangerous, stating that "this uncomplicated validation of law enforcement, while common in popular culture, is disturbing" given the ongoing violence against police and persons of color (Giovannone). The problematic endorsement continues throughout the series.

In Season Three, Hopper confronts a Russian operative, and the operative, despite having a gun to his head, does not believe Hopper will shoot. When questioned, the operative said he is not afraid because Hopper is a police officer, and police officers are required to follow the rules. In response, suggesting he is more than willing to break those rules, Hopper scoffs, "You want to test that theory?" ("Chapter Five: The Flayed"). Despite demonstrating in this scene that police sometimes abuse their power, Hopper is still a lovable character for most viewers, because he is an integral ally to the children and Joyce in each of the seasons as well as Eleven's adopted father. Regardless of his faults, audiences are trained to like and feel sympathy for him. When Hopper does break the rules, he does so to fight the bad guys, not because of any sort of bias. There is little to no discussion of the systemic racism embedded within the government, the primary concern flanking the Black Lives Matters movement.

This is not to say, however, that *Stranger Things* supports a color-blind racial ideology that ignores that race and racism exist. While *Stranger Things* does not examine the complicated relationship between law enforcement and persons of color, the Duffer Brothers do examine race relations between peers, ultimately offering positive representations of two persons of color: Lucas (Seasons One through Three) and Erica (Season Three). With Lucas the Duffer brothers avoid the token black friend stereotype, ensuring he has a more central role in the series. Over the three seasons his role was increasingly expanded to be more central to the plot.

The Duffer brothers not only expand the Lucas role but also explicitly address the lack of meaty roles for actors of color in the 1980s (and still today). In Season Two, when the boys dress up as characters from the movie *Ghostbusters*, Mike assumes that Lucas will be Winston, the one black character in the movie. Lucas, however, calls out Mike for suggesting he should play Winston, noting Mike is likely only making this suggestion because of his skin color. Lucas states, "I specifically didn't agree to Winston. No one wants to be Winston, man. . . . He joined the team super late, he's not funny, and he's not even a scientist" ("Chapter Two: Trick or Treat, Freak"). Lucas then proceeds to ask Mike if he thought he should play Winston because he is black. During this exchange, Lucas reiterates that he is just as smart as everyone else in the group; thus, he is just as deserving to be the smart, multidimensional Venkman.

This is an important exchange not only in regard to the series, but also in the greater context of 1980s popular culture. Ernie Hudson, the black actor cast to play Winston in *Ghostbusters*, recently expressed his disappointment with the character. When Hudson first read the script, he was excited at the opportunity. Winston, a complex character, was in the Air Force and an expert in demolition. After shooting began, however, some rewrites were made, and most of them erased anything compelling about the character. The changes made to his character, the only primary character of color in the movie, left the character flat and unimportant. In regard to the rewrites, Hudson explained: "The character was gone. Instead of coming in at the very beginning of the movie, like page 8, the character came in on page 68 after the Ghostbusters were established. His elaborate background was all gone, replaced by me walking in and saying, 'If there's a steady paycheck in it, I'll believe anything you say.' So that was pretty devastating." In addition to having minimal scenes, the character was not part of the trailer and was not on the movie poster, so it makes sense that Lucas would not want to be Winston for Halloween. *Stranger Things'* executive producer Dan Cohen explains why this scene is important: "Everyone's favorite character back then was Venkman. . . . It felt like a very natural thing for those kids to go through and Lucas has every right to not be that character if he doesn't want to" (Vick). Given this discussion in Season Two and the backstory of the making of *Ghostbusters*, it is appropriate that it is Lucas who grabs the grocery store fireworks, arguing the best way to defeat the mind flayer is to fight it with firepower. His idea proves critical, ultimately saving the town of Hawkins.

The Duffer brothers not only have Lucas be a key component to defeating the monster in Season Three; they also make him multidimensional by developing a relationship with him and Max, a redheaded girl in his class. This choice allowed them to further explore racial tensions in small-town America in an implicit way. In Season Two, when Lucas pursues Max, the Duffer brothers deviate from their source material. While 1980s film generally did not explore racial angst, certainly not in coming-of-age films, the brothers chose to highlight the tension of interracial dating in the 1980s. The Duffer brothers did not ignore the possibility of outcry over such a union, exploring it implicitly. Max's brother, Billy, is used to highlight this struggle. Megan Vick, writer for *TV Guide*, writes:

> The series made the more subtle move of positioning Max's stepbrother Billy (Dacre Montgomery) as the primary roadblock to Max and Lucas' budding relationship. Billy never out-and-out said he doesn't want Max hanging out with a black kid, but his unnatural aggression toward Lucas throughout the season, culminating in a physical attack in the finale, showed the danger of Lucas pursuing his crush in a way his friends would never and will never have to think about.

While the Duffer brothers could have overlooked the difficulties of interracial dating altogether, citing their desire to remain "true" to their source material, material in which race is relatively absent, they chose to highlight the prejudices interracial couples faced by using Billy as the vehicle.

Additionally, Lucas's sister, Erica, is one of the primary characters in Season Three. She plays a crucial role in the season, as she helps Steve, Robin, and Dustin fight the Russians and eventually the mind flayer. What makes her character unique is that not only is she crucial to the plot but also that, like her brother, she defies stereotypes. It is clear through her conversations with Dustin that she is smart and, well, a nerd. As noted earlier, this is not often the case for female characters in the 1980s (or even today)—and most certainly not female characters of color. While the series fails to address the systemic bias the Black Lives Matter movement seeks to highlight, it does diverge from 1980s stereotypes, refusing to shy away from all discussions in regard to race. As noted above, this is done via the characters of Lucas and Erica and via the relationship between Lucas and Max.

This Is America: Gen X Today

A lot has happened since the 1980s dataset was released during Gen X's adolescence. In some ways, the world is vastly different, particularly in regard to technology and how children are raised; in other ways it is the same, namely the economic and political climate. It makes sense that both the similarities and differences are reflected in *Stranger Things* because popular culture, as outlined throughout this entire book, both generates and articulates our understanding of the world. For example, because of the continued economic turmoil throughout Gen X's lifetime, including several recessions, *Stranger Things* explores the effects of income inequality on different types of families, ultimately offering a cynical perspective of the American Dream, much like the 1980s dataset, but heightened. Because the economic uncertainty that plagued Gen X's childhood still very much exists, these fears are reflected in the series. In addition to critiquing the economy, this representation also reflects Gen X's feelings toward their parents, namely their parents' shortcomings—including divorce and prioritizing individual fulfillment. Their childhood familial experiences have very much shaped how Gen Xers view family. While one might expect Gen X to use their cynicism to further erode the institution, for example, to shun marriage altogether, Gen X has used their cynicism in a completely different manner. They fought to restore the integrity of the institution, including expanding the notion of what constitutes a family. This is one reason why diverse families are celebrated, although not valorized, in *Stranger Things*.

In this chapter, I have outlined how *Stranger Things* diverges from the 1980s dataset, reflecting not only how Gen X viewed institutions in the 1980s as children and teenagers but also how Gen Xers view institutions in 2020 as adults. Specifically, I examine how three large cultural movements in the last decade are influenced the series: Occupy Wall Street, Me Too, and Black Lives Matter. Despite being a period piece, these three movements inform the series in unique ways, particularly in Seasons Two and Three, as the Duffer brothers substantially tweaked traditional 1980s tropes (e.g., creating female characters with more and resisting the token friend of color stereotype).

The Duffer brothers' willingness to listen to fan feedback is likely one of the primary reasons for these changes, as noted by Bundel. Because of this, the series transcends the decade in which it is set. Interestingly, the series still works as a slice of nostalgia for those watching, however, as it reflects Gen X's feelings toward these key institutions at different stages of their lifetime. This is what the series pays homage too, not simply 1980s popular culture (although, of course, that is part of the appeal).

Specifically, in this chapter, I have explored how the series addresses intersectionality and to what degree, via Karen and Joyce, and to a lesser extent, Jonathan and Nancy. I demonstrate how the series addresses issues regarding gender equality, paying particular attention in Season Three to giving its female characters' agency—fairly uncommon within the 1980s dataset. Additionally, via Lucas and Erica, the series offers positive representations of children of color that do not adhere to common stereotypes of the time period (and even today). Despite these positive representations and the numerous representations of law enforcement and government officials, the series fails to examine and critique the relationships between people of color and law enforcement, a primary focus of the Black Lives Matters movement. While each of these movements clearly influenced *Stranger Things*, in-depth social critiques are limited as the Duffer brothers clearly aim to retain the feel of 1980s coming-of-age movies.

Next I offer some concluding thoughts; how does the series, despite being influenced by current cultural movements, remain an ode to the 1980s? Why and how does it serve as a slice of nostalgia for so many viewers? In the conclusion, I argue that it is not simply an ode to a decade of popular culture and excess, but rather an ode to the generation that came of age during the decade: Gen X. Yes, there are numerous intertextual moments that any child of the 1980s would appreciate; however, throughout the series, the most prolific motif is that there is danger, which can come from both outside and from within. This is what binds each season together and resonates with audiences, specifically Gen X audiences. This danger reflects and influences Gen X's continued cynicism toward key American institutions.

Conclusion

In the 1989 movie *Heathers*, Winona Ryder says to her friend, "What's your damage, Heather?" (*Heathers*). The phrase quickly became popular, frequently used by Gen Xers as a way to sarcastically ask what person's mood or problem is. In the case of Gen X, the damage was clear. Throughout the 1980s dataset and *Stranger Things*, one of the overarching themes is that no person is safe, as danger can come from both outside and from within. The danger from the outside, for the most part, is evident: loss of one's physical or figurative home, financial stress from the widening income gap, or falling victim to criminal acts. Perhaps more surprising for viewers, however, is the danger that resides within. This danger is evident not only in regard to family (rising divorce rates and toxic family dynamics), but also in regard to the economy (the impact of the suburban sprawl and mindless conspicuous consumption) and government (inept or corrupt local and national agents). These dangers are seen in real life and then echoed in popular culture. They intersect with one another; for example, as noted, the economy can impact family dynamics. Many of the above factors, and the institutional erosion that followed, is likely what bred and reinforced a trust-no-one mentality in

Gen Xers, resulting in widespread skepticism and a largely disenfranchised generational cohort. Coming-of-age Gen Xers learned as children about these vulnerabilities from within and shrouded themselves in cynicism for protection, protection they were not guaranteed from the authority figures—parents, teachers, principals—in their lives.

As noted in chapter 5, however, their childhood and teenage cynicism did not cause adult Gen Xers to turn a blind eye to these institutions; rather, we see middle-aged Gen Xers working quietly to restore and redefine them, particularly the family unit. With divorce rates declining, Gen Xers have succeeded, at least in part, in changing some of the toxic family dynamics they experienced as adolescents. They found a source of pride in fixing and restoring what their parents broke or could not fix. Additionally, adult Gen Xers have worked as individuals and with peers to overcome a variety of obstacles, including several recessions, understanding that peers within even the most tarnished institutions are capable of doing good. This belief is reflected in *Stranger Things* and partially explains how and why the series diverges from the 1980s dataset used to flank this study. Within the 1980s dataset, there are no examples in which institutions and their agents are given opportunities for redemption. In *Stranger Things*, the moments of redemption reflect more nuanced views of each of these institutions and their agents. In part, this nuance comes from maturity (age), but also, key cultural movements of the last two decades (Occupy Wall Street, Me Too, and Black Lives Matter, all of which were experienced—and sometimes led—by Gen Xers) shaped Gen X's adult experiences and have influenced popular culture, including period pieces like *Stranger Things*.

One of the more memorable moments in *Stand by Me* reflects Gen X's complicated relationship with institutions. It demonstrates not only the ugliness that can reside within small communities but also Gen X's response to it. It shows how Gen Xers seek to expose corruption, seeing the need to tear down an institution in order to save it. This typically involves working together in order to do so. In *Stand by Me*, the scene takes place when the boys are sitting around a campfire after a long day of hiking. Gordie, an inspiring writer, tells a story. The story he shares is about an overweight boy, nicknamed Lardass, who is continually picked on and let down by others. In order to get back at his bullies, he drinks castor oil before participating in a pie-eating contest. His revenge, to disrupt a town tradition, an institution in his community, is to eat so much he vomits. It works. After Lardass vomits, so do others, leading to pure chaos in the crowd where, women "barfed all over the benevolent order of antelopes" (*Stand by Me*).

While this scene may seem like an adolescent gag inserted into a serious coming-of-age movie (and to a certain extent it is), it also summarizes Gen X's relationship with established customs, practices, and law. After being let down by institutions throughout their lifetime—family, the economy, and the government—many Gen Xers decided to go their own way. Lardass disrupts a time-honored tradition because it needed to be done. It needed to be done to show the ugly underbelly. The story ends with nearly everyone at the event throwing up, so we never see the resolution. Did this disruption—exposing the flawed and corrupt system—benefit the town? After Gordie finishes the story, Teddy wants to know what happened next for Lardass. He whines, "Geez, that ending sucks! Why don't you make it so that . . . so that Lardass goes home and he shoots his father, then he runs away an', and he joins the Texas Rangers. How about that?" (*Stand by Me*). Gordie brushes him off, and for good reason: the disruption is the point. What happens after, for Gen Xers, is done quietly and often together with little fanfare. This echoes how, in the midst of decay and despite cynicism, institutions are being shaped by Gen Xers, similar to how the children in *Stranger Things* quietly fight the shadow monster and mind flayer while the rest of the town remains oblivious.

Gen Xers in adulthood chose not to abandon the institutions as a whole but rather to attempt to disrupt and restructure them. As noted in chapter 2, they worked to redefine the family unit. As noted in chapter 3, they persevered despite a widening income gap. As noted in chapter 4, they worked together to find justice. They did not dismiss the institutions altogether; rather, they worked to change their relationship with them. They decided to live life their way, and this attitude is ultimately reflected in both the 1980s dataset (a reflection of young Gen X) and *Stranger Things* (a reflection of middle-aged Gen X).

Throughout this book, I have cited many popular culture writers and scholars. Many of these writers and scholars argue that *Stranger Things* serves as a tribute to the 1980s because of how the series references, parallels, and/or parodies the decade's most admired popular culture. I could have written an entire book (and I am sure there are several in the works) that outlines 1980s popular culture Easter eggs embedded within the series. They are too numerous to list and beyond the scope of this project. I would argue that while the references are numerous, rewarding audiences for their intertextual pop culture knowledge (particularly Gen X audiences), the series embodies the decade well beyond its aesthetic nods to pop culture. *Stranger Things* is similar to iconic 1980s films such as *The Breakfast Club*, *Ferris Bueller's Day Off*, and *The Goonies* not because of analogous characters or plotlines but because it reflects Gen X values, similar to the scene described above in *Stand by Me*. The focus of my work is namely to chronicle how *Stranger Things* reflects Gen X's perception of three key institutions. In addition to the 1980s aesthetics and popular culture references, this is why, for many Gen Xers, the series is a fulfilling slice of nostalgia. This is why it feels so real, so authentic.

In each of the seasons, it is clear that *Stranger Things* honors the 1980s by paying homage to the generation that grew up in and was shaped by it. The series nods to that generation not simply by recreating its youth but also by infusing the series with plotlines that very much reflect key large cultural movements of Gen X's adulthood, including movements that have influenced middle-aged Gen Xers. Within the 1980s dataset and *Stranger Things*, we see how Gen X's limited opportunities, distrust in authority, and financial strife sharpened the generation's distrust in institutions and anything that is considered traditional or normal, echoing a sentiment uttered by Jonathan in Season One of *Stranger Things*: "Nobody normal accomplished anything in this world" ("Chapter One: Madmax"). In addition to depicting Gen X's cynicism, in all of these artifacts we also see the independence and perseverance of Gen X, two of the characteristics used by Gen Xers to describe their generation. While they may have been forgotten in the eyes of the public, they were far from lost. The narrator in *Stand by Me* delivers one of the greatest descriptions of Gen X: "We knew exactly who we were and exactly where we were going. It was grand" (*Stand by Me*). My analysis shows just that. Gen X has always been mindful of its movements, and these movements, given Gen X's love of popular culture, is often reflected there. Ultimately, these aspects are what make *Stranger Things* a slice of sweet nostalgia for viewers—not the pop culture Easter eggs sprinkled throughout. This is why *Stranger Things* is so quintessentially 1980s: it is an ode to X.

Notes

Chapter 1. You're the Inspiration: Gen X and *Stranger Things*

1. "Feature Film, Released between 1980-01-01 and 1989-12-31 (Sorted by Number of Votes Descending)," Internet Movie Database (IMDb.com). https://www.imdb.com/search/title/?release_date=1980,1989&title_type=feature&sort=num_votes,desc.

2. Some would consider the Duffer brothers part of the Millennial generation; the time frame, however, is hotly contested, and many born in the early 1980s identify as Gen Xers.

Works Cited

"*Stranger Things* to Once Again Go Bump in the Night." *CBS Sunday Morning,* 20 August 2017. www.cbsnews.com/news/stranger-things -to-once-again-go-bump-in-the-night/.

Andersen, Kurt. "Kurt Andersen on the 1980s, Our Nation's Manic Episode." *Vanity Fair,* 30 August 2015. https://www.vanityfair.com /culture/2013/10/kurt-andersen-on-the-1980s.

Arnett, Jeffrey Jensen. "High Hopes in a Grim World: Emerging Adults' Views of Their Futures and 'Generation X.'" *Youth & Society* 31, no. 3 (2000): 267–86.

Auxier, Richard. "Reagan's Recession." *Pew Research Center,* 14 December 2010. http://www.pewresearch.org/2010/12/14/reagans -recession/.

Back to the Future. Directed by Robert Zemeckis. Universal Pictures, 1985.

Back to the Future Part II. Directed by Robert Zemeckis. Universal Pictures, 1989.

Baker, Lucy, and Amanda Howell. "Parenting into the Spin: Trauma, Coming of Age, and Raising Children in *Stranger Things.*" *Refractory: A Journal of Entertainment Media* 31 (2019). https:// refractory-journal.com/parenting-into-the-spin-trauma-coming-of -age-and-raising-children-in-stranger-things/. Accessed 20 May 2019.

Beschloss, Michael. "The Ad That Helped Reagan Sell Good Times to an Uncertain Nation." *New York Times,* 7 May 2016. https://

www.nytimes.com/2016/05/08/business/the-ad-that-helped
-reagan-sell-good-times-to-an-uncertain-nation.html.

Behr, Peter. "Is It All Downhill from Here? The Case of the Missing
Productivity; Despite Computers, Faxes, Service Sector Output
Lags." *Washington Post*, 21 January 1990 (Sunday, Final Edition),
H1. LexisNexis Academic. Web. Accessed 25 September 2017.

Big. Directed by Penny Marshall. American Entertainment Partners
II, 1988.

Bogost, Ian. "When Malls Saved Suburbia from Despair." *The Atlantic*,
17 February 2018. https://www.theatlantic.com/technology/archive
/2018/02/when-malls-saved-cities-from-capitalism/553610/.

Boudreau, Brenda. "Badass Mothers: Challenging Nostalgia." *Uncovering Stranger Things: Essays on Eighties Nostalgia, Cynicism and
Innocence in the Series*, edited by Kevin J. Wetmore Jr., 164–72. Jefferson, NC: McFarland, 2018.

The Breakfast Club. Directed by John Hughes. Universal Pictures, 1985.

Beutell, Nicholas J., and Ursula Wittig-Berman. "Work-family Conflict and Work-family Synergy for Generation X, Baby Boomers,
and Matures: Generational Differences, Predictors, and Satisfac-
tion Outcomes." *Journal of Managerial Psychology* 23, no. 5 (2008):
507–23.

Bundel, Ani. "Netflix's 'Stranger Things' Season Three Is Growing Up,
Pushing Boundaries and Having Fun." *NBC News*, 4 July 2019.
http://www.nbcnews.com/think/opinion/netflix-s-stranger-things
-season-three-growing-pushing-boundaries-having-ncna1026461.

Butler, Rose. "The Eaten-for-Breakfast Club: Teenage Nightmares in
Stranger Things." *Uncovering Stranger Things: Essays on Eighties
Nostalgia, Cynicism and Innocence in the Series*, edited by Kevin J.
Wentmore Jr., 72–83. Jefferson, NC: McFarland, 2018.

Carnevale, Anthony. "Trickle Down and Out; Low-Tech Reality:
How Workers Get Hurt in Our Flexible Economy." *Washington
Post*, 27 November 1994 (Sunday, Final Edition), C3. LexisNexis
Academic. Web. Accessed 25 September 2017.

Carranza, Ashley Jae. "The Rebirth of King's Children." *Uncovering
Stranger Things: Essays on Eighties Nostalgia, Cynicism and Inno-
cence in the Series*, edited by Kevin J. Wentmore Jr., 8–19. Jefferson,
NC: McFarland, 2018.

Carruthers, Elsa M. "Revisiting the Monstrous Feminine and Monster Parents in *Stranger Things*." *Uncovering Stranger Things: Essays on Eighties Nostalgia, Cynicism and Innocence in the Series*, edited by Kevin J. Wentmore Jr., 128–34. Jefferson, NC: McFarland, 2018.

"Chapter Eight: The Battle of Starcourt." *Stranger Things*, season 3, episode 8. Netflix, 4 July 2019. https://www.netflix.com/title/80057281.

"Chapter Five: Dig Dug." *Stranger Things*, season 2, episode 5. Netflix, 27 October 2017. http://www.netflix.com/title/80057281.

"Chapter Five: The Flayed." *Stranger Things*, season 3, episode 5. Netflix, 4 July 2019. https://www.netflix.com/title/80057281.

"Chapter Five: The Flea and the Acrobat." *Stranger Things*, season 1, episode 5. Netflix, 15 July 2016. https://www.netflix.com/title/80057281.

"Chapter Four: The Sauna Test." *Stranger Things*, season 3, episode 4. Netflix, 4 July 2019. https://www.netflix.com/title/80057281.

"Chapter Four: Will the Wise." *Stranger Things*, season 4, episode 9. Netflix, 27 October 2017. https://www.netflix.com/title/80057281.

"Chapter Nine: The Gate." *Stranger Things*, season 2, episode 9. Netflix, 27 October 2017. https://www.netflix.com/title/80057281.

"Chapter One: MADMAX." *Stranger Things*, season 2, episode 1. Netflix, 27 October 2017. https://www.netflix.com/title/80057281.

"Chapter One: Suzie, Do You Copy?" *Stranger Things*, season 3, episode 1. Netflix, 4 July 2019. https://www.netflix.com/title/80057281.

"Chapter One: The Vanishing of Will Byers." *Stranger Things*, season 1, episode 1. Netflix, 15 July 2016. https://www.netflix.com/title/80057281.

"Chapter Six: E Pluribus Unum." *Stranger Things*, season 3, episode 6. Netflix, 4 July 2019. https://www.netflix.com/title/80057281.

"Chapter Six: The Spy." *Stranger Things*, season 2, episode 6. Netflix, 27 October 2017. https://www.netflix.com/title/80057281.

"Chapter Seven: The Bathtub." *Stranger Things*, season 1, episode 7. Netflix, 15 July 2016. https://www.netflix.com/title/80057281.

"Chapter Seven: The Bite." *Stranger Things*, season 3, episode 7. Netflix, 4 July 2019. https://www.netflix.com/title/80057281.

"Chapter Seven: The Lost Sister." *Stranger Things*, season 2, episode 7. Netflix, 27 October 2017. https://www.netflix.com/title/80057281.

"Chapter Three: The Case of the Missing Lifeguard." *Stranger Things*, season 3, episode 3. Netflix, 4 July 2019. https://www.netflix.com /title/80057281.

"Chapter Three: Holly, Jolly." *Stranger Things*, season 1, episode 3. Netflix, 15 July 2016. https://www.netflix.com/title/80057281.

"Chapter Three: The Pollywog." *Stranger Things*, season 2, episode 3. Netflix, 27 October 2017. https://www.netflix.com/title/80057281.

"Chapter Two: The Mall Rats." *Stranger Things*, season 3, episode 2. Netflix, 4 July 2019. https://www.netflix.com/title/80057281.

"Chapter Two: Trick or Treat, Freak." *Stranger Things*, season 2, episode 2. Netflix, 27 October 2017. https://www.netflix.com/title /80057281.

Coleman, Marilyn J., and Lawrence H. Ganong. *The Social History of the American Family: An Encyclopedia*. Thousand Oaks, CA: Sage, 2014.

"The Country-Club Vote." *The Economist*, 18 May 2000. https://www .economist.com/united-states/2000/05/18/the-country-clubvo.

Coupland, Douglas. "Generation X'd." *Details* (June 1995). http:// coupland.tripod.com/details1.html.

Coupland, Douglas. *Generation X: Tales for an Accelerated Culture*. New York: St. Martin's Press, 1991.

Currier, Erin. "How Generation X Could Change the American Dream." *Trend*, 26 January 2018. https://trend.pewtrusts.org/en /archive/winter-2018/how-generation-x-could-change-the -american-dream.

D'Addario, Daniel. "Review: Stranger Things Is Nostalgia That Works." *Time*, 14 July 2016. www.time.com/4406854/review -stranger-things-is-nostalgia-that-works/.

Da Silva, Chantal. "Has Occupy Wall Street Changed America?" *Newsweek*, 19 September 2018. http://www.newsweek.com/has -occupy-wall-street-changed-america-seven-years-birth-political -movement-1126364.

Davis, Holly [@hollymdavis]. "I'm #GenX. I just sit on the sidelines and watch the world burn. -#keenanthompson @nbcsnl." Twitter, 20 January 2019. https://twitter.com/hollymdavis/status/10868 51716799258624.

Dead Poets Society. Directed by Peter Weir. Touchstone Pictures, 1989.

Delgado, Michelle. "The Deeper Significance of the Mall on *Stranger Things*." *The Atlantic*, 17 July 2019. http://www.theatlantic.com /entertainment/archive/2019/07/significance-stranger-things-3s -starcourt-mall/594106/.

Dickson, EJ. "Five Reasons 'Stranger Things' Isn't the Feminist Show of Your Dreams." *Mic*, 5 August 2016. https://www.mic.com /articles/150689/5-reasons-why-stranger-things-isn-t-the-feminist -show-of-our-dreams.

Donegan, Moira. "How #MeToo Revealed the Central Rift within Feminism Today." *The Guardian*, 11 May 2018. https://www.the guardian.com/news/2018/may/11/how-metoo-revealed-the -central-rift-within-feminism-social-individualist.

D'Souza, Joy. "Xennials, The Microgeneration Between Gen X and Millennials." *Huffington Post*, 28 June 2017. www.huffingtonpost .ca/2017/06/28/xennials_a_23006562/.

Duke, Lynn. "Video Games Blast Off in Popularity Series." *St. Petersburg Times*, 2 July 1989. ProQuest. Accessed 25 October 2018.

Ellin, Abby. "Preludes: A Generation of Freelancers." *New York Times*, 15 August 1999. http://www.nytimes.com/1999/08/15/business /preludes-a-generation-of-freelancers.html.

E.T. the Extra-Terrestrial. Directed by Steven Spielberg. Universal Pictures, 1982.

Featherstone, Liza. "Talkin' 'Bout Their Generation." *Columbia Journalism Review* (July/August 1994): 40–42.

Ferris Bueller's Day Off. Directed by John Hughes. Paramount Pictures, 1986.

Feuer, Jane. "Genre Study and Television." *Channel of Discourse Reassembled: Television and Contemporary Criticism*, edited by Robert C. Allen, 138–59. New York: Routledge, 1992.

"Flyover: The Myth of a 'Bootstraps' America." *Flyover*, MPR News, 17 September 2017. https://www.flyoverradio.org.

Framke, Caroline. "'Stranger Things' Finally Does Right by Female Characters with Maya Hawke's Robin." *Variety*, 6 July 2019. http://variety.com/2019/tv/columns/stranger-things-season-3 -robin-steve-spoilers-1203259061/.

Franklin, Anthony David. "Half-Lives of the Nuclear Family: Representations of the Mid-Century American Family in *Stranger Things*." In *Uncovering Stranger Things: Essays on Eighties Nostalgia, Cynicism and Innocence in the Series*, edited by Kevin J. Wetmore Jr., 174–82. Jefferson, NC: McFarland, 2018.

Freeman, Heather. "Shifting Nostalgic Boundaries: Archetypes and Queer Representation in *Stranger Things*, *GLOW*, and *One Day at a Time*." In *Nostalgia: Streaming the Past on Demand*, edited by Kathryn Pallister, 91–108. New York: Lexington Books, 2019.

Fry, Richard. "Gen X Rebounds as the Only Generation to Recover the Wealth Lost after the Housing Crash." Pew Research Center, 23 July 2018. http://www.pewresearch.org/fact-tank/2018/07/23/gen-x-rebounds-as-the-only-generation-to-recover-the-wealth-lost-after-the-housing-crash/.

Fry, Richard, and Jeffrey Passell. "In Post-Recession Era, Young Adults Drive Continuing Rise in Multi-Generational Living." Pew Research Center, 14 July 2014. http://www.pewsocialtrends.org/2014/07/17/in-post-recession-era-young-adults-drive-continuing-rise-in-multi-generational-living.

Garvey, Anna. "The Oregon Trail Generation: Life Before and After Mainstream Tech." *Social Media Week*, 21 April 2015. http://socialmediaweek.org/blog/2015/04/oregon-trail-generation/.

"The Generation Gap in American Politics." Pew Research Center, 1 March 2018. http://www.people-press.org/2018/03/01/1-generations-party-identification-midterm-voting-preferences-views-of-trump/. Accessed 25 July 2019.

"Generation X." National and Community Service. https://www.nationalservice.gov/vcla/demographic/generation-x.

Gibson, Jane Whitney, Regina A. Greenwood, and Edward F. Murphy Jr. "Generational Differences in the Workplace: Personal Values, Behaviors, and Popular Beliefs." *Journal of Diversity Management* 4, no. 3 (2009): 1–8.

Gilbert, Sophie. "The American Paranoia of *Stranger Things 3*." *The Atlantic*, 4 July 2019. http://www.theatlantic.com/entertainment/archive/2019/07/stranger-things-3-american-paranoia-review/593185/?fbclid=IwAR3e3z-Zz_rpDPs3cNqnliSBYb6xun-fv6A9-HBpqi7L717ROqScMhkTSOM.

Giles, Jeff, and Susan Miller. "Generalizations X." *Newsweek*, 6 June 1994, 64–72.

Giovannone, Aaron. "Stranger Things 2 Relies on Nostalgic Race Politics." *The Conversation*, 2 January 2018. http://theconversation .com/stranger-things-2-relies-on-nostalgic-race-politics-89522.

Goldman, Eric. "Stranger Things: Season 1 Review." IGN, 8 July 2016. www.ign.com/articles/2016/07/08/stranger-things-season-1-review.

The Goonies. Directed by Richard Donner, Warner Bros., 1985.

Gordinier, Jeff. *X Saves the World: How Generation X Got the Shaft but Can Still Keep Everything from Sucking*. New York: Penguin, 2008.

Gozzi, Raymond, Jr. "The Generation X and Boomers Metaphors." *ETC: A Review of General Semantics* 52, no. 3 (1995): 331–35.

Grant, Barry Keith. *The Hollywood Film Musical*. West Sussex, UK: Wiley-Blackwell, 2012.

Gremlins. Directed by Joe Dante. Warner Bros., 1984.

Grimes, Maiasia. "A Feminist Critique of Netflix's Stranger Things." Odyssey, 12 September 2016. https://www.theodysseyonline.com /feminist-critique-netflixs-stranger.

Groom, Kia. "The Stranger Sex: Subverting Gendered Tropes in *Stranger Things*." The Mary Sue, 16 August 2016. https://www.the marysue.com/the-stranger-sex-subverting-gendered-tropes-in -stranger-things/.

Grossberg, Lawrence. "Cinema, Postmodernity and Authenticity." In *Movie Music: The Film Reader*, edited by Kay Dickinson, 83–97. New York: Taylor & Francis, 2003.

Halstead, Ted. "A Politics for Generation X." *The Atlantic*, August 1999. http://www.theatlantic.com/magazine/archive/1999/08/a -politics-for-generation-x/306666/.

Hanson, Peter. *The Cinema of Generation X: A Critical Study of Films and Directors*. Jefferson, NC: McFarland, 2002.

Heathers. Directed by Michael Lehmann. Arrow Films, 1989.

Heba, Gary. "Everyday Nightmares." *Journal of Popular Film and Television* 23, no. 3 (1995): 106–15.

Hogan, Mark. "The Rise of the Evil Developers." *Vulture*, 23 December 2017. https://www.citylab.com/life/2017/12/real-estate-tycoons-are -the-ultimate-movie-villains/547433/.

Hornblower, Margot. "Great Xpectations of So-Called Slackers." *Time*, 9 June 1997, 58–68.

"How Groups Voted in 1984." Roper Center for Public Opinion Research, 2019. http://ropercenter.cornell.edu/how-groups-voted-1984.

Howe, Neil, and Bill Strauss. *13th Gen: Abort, Retry, Ignore, Fail?* New York: Vintage, 1993.

Howe, Neil, and William Strauss. *Millennials Rising: The Next Great Generation*. New York: Vintage, 2009.

Howe, Neil, and William Strauss. "The Next 20 Years: How Customer and Workforce Attitudes Will Evolve." *Harvard Business Review* 85, nos. 7–8 (2007): 41–52.

Hudson, Ernie. "The Painful What-If that Haunts 'Ghostbuster' Ernie Hudson." *Entertainment Weekly*, 5 November 2014. http://ew.com/article/2014/11/05/ghostbusters-ernie-hudson/.

Huntington, Samuel P. "The U.S.—Decline or Renewal?" *Foreign Affairs* 67, no. 2 (Winter 1988/89): 76–96.

Hurlin, Tara. "Call in Sick: The Cars of Ferris Bueller's Day Off," Hagerty, 10 June 2016. https://www.hagerty.com/articles-videos/articles/2016/06/10/ferris-bueller.

Jackson, Gregory A., and George S. Masnick. "Take Another Look at Regional U.S. Growth." *Harvard Business Review* 61, no. 2 (1983): 76–87.

Jenkins, Henry. *Convergence Culture: Where Old and New Media Collide*. New York: New York University Press, 2008.

"The K Car: Variations on a Theme Helped to Save Chrysler." *New York Times*, 29 January 1984. https://www.nytimes.com/1984/01/29/automobiles/the-k-car-variations-on-a-theme-helped-to-save-chrysler.html

Kidd, Dustin. *Pop Culture Freaks: Identity, Mass Media, and Society*, 2nd ed. New York: Routledge, 2019.

Kiesa, Abby, et al. "Millennials Talk Politics: A Study of College Student Political Engagement." Center for Information and Research on Civic Learning and Engagement, 2007. https://eric.ed.gov/?id=ED498899. Accessed 12 March 2019.

King, James. *The Ultimate History of the '80s Teen Movie*. New York: Diversion Books, 2019.

Kitwana, Bakari. *The Hip Hop Generation*. New York: Basic Civitas, 2002.

Lavin, Cheryl. "People Born Between 1961 and 1981 Are . . ." *Chicago Tribune*, 13 June 1993. https://www.chicagotribune.com/news/ct -xpm-1993–06–13–9306130204-story.html.

Litt, Toby. "The 80s: The Best of Times, the Worst of Times." *The Guardian*, 29 July 2010. https://www.theguardian.com/film/2010 /jul/29/80s-culture-a-team-karate-kid.

Livingston, Gretchen. "The Changing Profile of Unmarried Parents." Pew Research Center, 25 April 2018. http://www.pewsocialtrends .org/2018/04/25/the-changing-profile-of-unmarried-parents/.

Lussier, Germain, Cheryl Eddy, Beth Elderkin, and Charles Pulliam- Moore. "17 Things We Loved about *Stranger Things 3* (And 6 We Didn't)." Gizmodo, 9 July 2019. https://io9.gizmodo.com/17- things -we-loved-about-stranger-things-3-and-6-we-di-1836027390.

MacNamara, Jim. *The 21st Century Media [R]evolution*, 2nd ed. New York: Peter Lang, 2014.

Madonna. "Material Girl." *Like a Virgin*. LP/CD, Warner Bros., 1985.

Malacarne, Timothy. "Rich Friends, Poor Friends: Inter-Socioeco- nomic Status Friendships in Secondary School." *Socius* 3 (2017). https://doi.org/10.1177/2378023117736994.

Martin, Anna Sofia. "The Undetected Influence Of Generation X." *Forbes*, 16 September 2018. https://www.forbes.com/sites/next avenue/2016/09/13/the-undetected-influence-of-generation-x /#357672191efb.

Masibigiri, Vhutshilo, and Hester Nienaber. "Factors Affecting the Retention of Generation X Public Servants: An Exploratory Study." *SA Journal of Human Resource Management* 9, no. 1 (2011). https://sajhrm.co.za/index.php/sajhrm/article/view/318/304. Accessed 12 March 2019.

Mazza, Ed. "Generation Xers Have the Most Gen X Response to Being Left Off the List." Huffington Post, 19 January 2019. https://www.huffpost.com/entry/generation-x-forgotten-again_n _5c4539d5e4b027c3bbc2fc87.

McKeage, Kim K. R. "Materialism and Self-Indulgences: Themes of Materialism in Self-Gift Giving." In *Meaning, Measure, and*

Morality of Materialism, edited by Floyd W. Rudmin and Marsha Richins, 140–46. Provo, UT: Association for Consumer Research, 1992.

McVey, Ciara. "'Stranger Things' Star Natalia Dyer Opens Up about Sexual Discrimination Storyline in Season 3." *Hollywood Reporter*, 8 July 2019. http://www.hollywoodreporter.com/news/stranger -things-star-natalia-dyer-nancys-sexual-discrimination-season-3 -watch-1222892.

McWilliams, Dean. "American Film Production in the 1980s." *Constructing the Eighties: Versions of an American Decade*, edited by Walter Grünzweig, Roberta Maierhofer, and Adolf Wimmer, 97–108. Tübingen, Germany: Gunter Narr Verlag, 1992.

"Millennials." National and Community Service. http://www.national service.gov/vcla/demographic/generation-x.

Miller, Ryan W. "Are you a Xennial? How to Tell If You're the Microgeneration Between Gen X and Millenial." *USA Today*, 20 December 2018. http://www.usatoday.com/story/news/nation /2018/12/20/xennials-millennials-generation-x-microgeneration /2369230002/.

Mittell, Jason. "A Cultural Approach to Television Genre Theory." *Cinema Journal* 43, no. 3 (2001): 3–24.

Mollet, T. "Looking Through the Upside Down: Hyperpostmodernism and Trans-mediality in the Duffer Brothers' *Stranger Things* Series." *Journal of Popular Television* 7, no. 1 (2019): 57–77.

Morton, Lisa. "Not a Princess Anymore: How the Casting of Winona Ryder in *Stranger Things* Speaks to the Essential Falsehood of 1980s Media Depictions of the American Working Class." In *Uncovering Stranger Things: Essays on Eighties Nostalgia, Cynicism and Innocence in the Series*, edited by Kevin J. Wentmore Jr., 93–102. Jefferson, NC: McFarland, 2018.

Myers, David S. "Editorials on the Economy in the 1980 Presidential Campaign." *Journalism Quarterly* 59, no. 3 (September 1982): 414–19.

Neal, Stephanie, and Richard Wellins. "Generation X—Not Millennials—Is Changing the Nature of Work." CNBC, 11 April 2018. https://www.cnbc.com/2018/04/11/generation-x—not -millennials—is-changing-the-nature-of-work.html.

Neale, Stephen. "Studying Genre." *The Television Genre Book*, edited by Glen Creeber, Toby Miller, and John Tulloch, 3–4. New York: Palgrave Macmillan, 2015.

Ngak, Chenda. "Occupy Wall Street Uses Social Media to Spread Nationwide." CBS News, 13 October 2017. http://www.cbsnews.com/news/occupy-wall-street-uses-social-media-to-spread-nationwide/.

A Nightmare on Elm Street. Directed by Wes Craven. New Line Cinema, 1984.

Oake, Jonathon I. "Reality Bites and Generation X as Spectator." *The Velvet Light Trap* 53 no.1 (2004): 83–97.

"Occupy Wall Street Movement Creates Rift among Gen X Crowd." *New Haven Register*, 18 December 2011. http://www.nhregister.com/news/article/Occupy-Wall-Street-movement-creates-rift-among-11574049.php.

O'Donovan, Cheryl. "The X Styles: Communication Styles of Gen Xers." *Communication World* 15, no. 1 (1997): 17–20.

"The Original Gen X." BBC, 1 March 2014. http://www.bbc.com/news/magazine-26339959.

Ortner, Sherry B. "Generation X: Anthropology in a Media-saturated World." *Cultural Anthropology* 13, no. 3 (1998): 414–40.

Oswalt, Patton [@pattonoswalt]. "As a member of Gen X, I am 100% cool with being left out of this mess." Twitter, 20 January 2019. https://twitter.com/pattonoswalt/status/1087177691084709889.

Owen, Rob. *Gen X TV: The Brady Bunch to Melrose Place*. Syracuse, NY: Syracuse University Press, 1997.

Pace, Tom. "'Will I Do Myself Proud or Only What's Allowed?' Performing Masculinities and Generation X Men in Contemporary Hollywood Comedies." *Interactions: Studies in Communication and Culture* 6, no. 3 (2015): 343–59.

Pace, Tom. "Portrait of the Xer as a White-Bred Suburbanite: *Mad Men* as a Generation X Understanding of the 1960s." *Generation X Professors Speak: Voices from Academia*, edited by Elwood Watson, 151–68. Lanham, MD: Scarecrow Press, 2013.

Parker, Kim, Nikki Graf, and Ruth Igielnik. "Generation Z Looks a Lot Like Millennials on Key Social and Political Issues." Pew Research Center, 17 January 2019. https://www.pewsocialtrends

.org/2019/01/17/generation-z-looks-a-lot-like-millennials-on-key
-social-and-political-issues/.

"Parenting in America." Pew Research Center, 15 September 2015.
http://www.pewsocialtrends.org/2015/12/17/1-the-american
-family-today/.

Pink Floyd. "Another Brick in the Wall (Part 2)." *The Wall*. LP,
Columbia, 1979.

Poindexter, Paula M., and Lasorsa, Dominic L. "Generation X: Is
Its Meaning Understood?" *Newspaper Research Journal* 20, no. 4
(1999): 28–36.

Ramanathan, Lavanya. "We Thought Gen X Was a Bunch of Slackers.
Now They're the Suits." *Washington Post*, 1 March 2017. https://
www.washingtonpost.com/lifestyle/style/we-thought-gen-x-was
-a-bunch-of-slackers-now-theyre-the-suits/2017/03/01/eba47346
-f924-11e6-9845-.

Rampell, Catherine. "The Other Way George H. W. Bush's Passing Was the End of an Era." *Washington Post*, 3 December 2018.
https://www.washingtonpost.com/opinions/george-hw-bush-was-
the-last-of-his-kind—a-republican-who-didnt-believe-in-voodoo
-economics/2018/12/03/25aa090a-f740-11e8-8c9a-860ce2a8148f
_story.html?noredirect=on&utm_term=.2e20be928afc.

Raphelson, Samantha. "From GIs to Gen Z (Or is it iGen?): How
Generations Get Nicknames." National Public Radio, 6 October
2014. https://www.npr.org/2014/10/06/349316543/don-t-label
-me-origins-of-generational-names-and-why-we-use-them.

Reagan, Ronald. "Address Before a Joint Session of Congress on the
State of the Union." American Presidency Project. https://www
.presidency.ucsb.edu/node/254269.

Riismandel, Kyle. "Arcade Addicts and Mallrats: Producing and
Policing Suburban Public Space in 1980s America." *Environment,
Space, Place* 5, no. 2 (2013): 65–89.

Rodriguez, Raul O., Mark T. Green, and Malcolm James Ree.
"Leading Generation X: Do the Old Rules Apply?" *Journal of
Leadership and Organizational Studies* 9, no. 4 (2003): 67–75.

Romano, Aja. "Season 3 Stranger Things Has Good Ideas but Poor
Execution." Vox, 4 July 2019. https://www.vox.com/culture/2019

/7/4/19413771/stranger-things-season-3-review-recap-hopper
-eleven-russians.

Rout, Cameron. "Stranger Things Is Way, Way, More Feminist Than
You Think." Medium, 17 December 2018. https://medium.com/@
cameronrout/stranger-things-is-way-way-more-feminist-than-you
-think-5f5a5abceae0.

Samuel, Lawrence R. *The American Dream: A Cultural History*. Syracuse, NY: Syracuse University Press, 2012.

Samuelson, Robert J. "A Frivolous Decade?" *Washington Post*, 3 January 1990, A15. LexisNexis Academic. Web. Accessed 25 September
2017.

Schladebeck, Jessica. "A Look at 'Stranger Things' and the Secret Government Experiments That Inspired It." *New York Daily News*, 1
September 2016. www.nydailynews.com/entertainment/tv/stranger
-inspired-secret-government-experiments-article-1.2774525.

Schwarz, John E., and Thomas J. Volgy. "The Myth of America's Economic Decline." *Harvard Business Review* 63, no. 5 (September/
October 1985): 98–107.

Scott, David Clark. "The Lure of Pac Man: Parents Voice Concern
over Video Game Centers." *Christian Science Monitor*, 12 October
1982. ProQuest. Accessed 25 October 2018.

Scibelli, Anthony. "The Anarchic Comedy of Joe Dante's 'Gremlins.'"
Vulture, 30 January 2013. https://www.vulture.com/2013/01/the
-anarchic-comedy-of-joe-dantes-gremlins.html.

Scribner, Sara. "Generation X Gets Really Old: How Do Slackers
Have a Midlife Crisis?" Salon, 11 August 2013. https://www.salon
.com/2013/08/11/generation_x_gets_really_old_how_do_slackers
_have_a_midlife_crisis/.

Shafrir, Doree. "Generation Catalano." Slate, 24 October 2001. www
.slate.com/articles/life/culturebox/2011/10/generation_catalano
_the_generation_stuck_between_gen_x_and_the_m.html.

Shary, Timothy. *Generation Multiplex: The Image of Youth in American Cinema Since 1980*. Austin: University of Texas Press, 2014.

Shugart, Helene A. "Isn't It Ironic? The Intersection of Third-Wave
Feminism and Generation X." *Women's Studies in Communication*
24, no. 2 (2001): 131–68.

Sirianni, Joseph M. "*Stranger Things* and the Pervasiveness of Nostalgic Television." In *Nostalgia: Streaming the Past on Demand*, edited by Kathryn Pallister, 185–102. Lanham, MD: Lexington Books, 2019.

Smith, Lacey N. "A Nice Home at the End of the Cul-de-sac: Hawkins as Infected Postmodern Suburbia." In *Uncovering Stranger Things: Essays on Eighties Nostalgia, Cynicism and Innocence in the Series*, edited by Kevin J. Wetmore Jr., 215–24. Jefferson, NC: McFarland, 2018.

Smokler, Kevin. "'Stranger Things' and the Sinister Innocence of Reagan's America." Salon, 24 October 2017. https://www.salon.com /2017/10/24/stranger-things-and-the-dubious-innocence-of -hawkins-indiana/.

Sourdot, Ludovic A. "The Upside Down of Education Reform During the Reagan Era: A Re-Examination of Education Policies Through Stranger Things." In *Uncovering Stranger Things: Essays on Eighties Nostalgia, Cynicism and Innocence in the Series*, edited by Kevin J. Wetmore Jr., 205–14. Jefferson, NC: McFarland, 2018.

Stern, Gabriella. "Cadillac Seeks Fountain of Youth Buyers." *Chicago Tribune*, 29 October 1995. https://www.chicagotribune.com/news /ct-xpm-1995-10-29-9510290165-story.html.

Stand by Me. Directed by Rob Reiner. Columbia Pictures, 1986.

Steinberg, Shirley R., and Joe L. Kincheloe. "Privileged and Getting Away with It: The Cultural Studies of White, Middle-class Youth." *Studies in the Literary Imagination* 31, no. 1 (1998): 103–26.

"Stranger Things." IMDb. http://www.imdb.com/title/tt4574334/ ?ref_=tttg_tg_tt. Accessed 25 July 2019.

Taylor, Paul. "The Next America: Boomers, Millennials, and the Looming Generational Showdown." Pew Research Center, 2014.

Taylor, Paul, and George Gao. "Generation X: America's Neglected 'Middle Child.'" Pew Research Center, 5 June 2014. http://www .pewresearch.org/fact-tank/2014/06/05/generation-x-americas -neglected-middle-child/.

Veblen, Thorstein. *The Theory of the Leisure Class*. New York: Macmillan, 1912.

Vernon, Steve. "Life Planning in the Age of Longevity." Stanford Center on Longevity, 2017. http://longevity.stanford.edu/wp-content/uploads/2018/05/Life-Planning-Gen-X.pdf.

Vick, Megan. "How *Stranger Things* Subverted the 'Token Black Kid' Trope." *TV Guide*, 16 November 2017. http://www.tvguide.com/news/stranger-things-subverted-token-black-kid-trope/.

Warshauer, Matthew. "Who Wants to Be a Millionaire: Changing Conceptions of the American Dream." AR Net, American Studies Resource Centre. http://www.americansc.org.uk/online/American_Dream.htm. Accessed 27 September 2017.

Watson, Elwood, ed. *Generation X Professors Speak: Voices from Academia*. Lanham, MD: Scarecrow Press, 2013.

Weinberg, Mark. "What I Learned Watching 'Back to the Future' with Ronald Reagan." *Politico*, 27 February 2018. https://www.politico.com/magazine/story/2018/02/27/ronald-reagan-press-aide-movie-nights-with-reagan-217095.

Will, George. "The Greatest Movie." *Washington Post*, 26 June 1986. http://www.washingtonpost.com/archive/opinions/1986/06/26/the-greatest-movie/829b4acb-5a06–4162-ab3e-369399199ed7/?utm_term=.6b0c2bef7c4b.

Williams, Alex. "Actually Gen X Did Sell Out, Invent All Things Millennial, and Cause Everything Else That Is Great and Awful." *New York Times*, 14 May 2019. https://www.nytimes.com/2019/05/14/style/gen-x-millenials.html.

Index

Adbusters, 130
American Dream, 8, 20, 60, 62,
    63, 67, 68, 90, 91, 95, 101,
    131, 156
American Myth, 60, 62, 64
arcades, 55–56

Baby Boomer generation, 3, 4,
    6, 7, 8, 45, 95, 105, 119, 124,
    131–32, 151
Back to the Future (Zemeckis),
    14, 27, 47–48, 50, 51, 67,
    84–85, 86, 87, 89, 95,
    100–101, 117–18; Biff,
    82; George, 30, 31, 82;
    Lorraine, 28, 30, 82; Marty,
    30, 47, 48, 82, 101
Back to the Future II (Zemeckis),
    14; Future Biff, 26, 31, 118;
    Future Doc, 53, 108; Future
    Lorraine, 31; Marty, 86,
    108, 118
Batteries Not Included (Robbins),
    66

Big (Marshall), 14, 36, 46, 47, 57,
    95; Josh, 36, 57, 69, 76–77
Black Lives Matter movement,
    125, 127, 151, 153, 156–58
Black Panther Party, 152
Breakfast Club, The (Hughes),
    14, 25–28, 51, 72, 76–77,
    80–81, 95, 137, 162; Allison,
    27, 28, 47, 81; Andrew,
    26–27, 49; Bender, 26–27;
    Claire, 27
Brin, Sergey, 9

Caddyshack (Ramis), 64
Caddyshack II (Arkush), 64
Capa, Robert, 4
Catalano Generation, 10
Clash, The (band), 30, 56
Clerks (Smith), 11
Cohen, Dan, 154
Coupland, Douglas, 4–5, 10

Dead Poets Society (Weir), 14, 25,
    51, 100, 101–2; Mr. Keating,

50, 52–53; Lorraine, 27–28;
Neil Perry's father, 26;
Perry family, 28, 30
Democrats, 148, 149
Dorsey, Jack, 9
Duffer, Matt, and Ross Duffer
(Duffer brothers), 15, 17,
20–21, 73–74, 89, 111, 115,
120, 121, 143, 145, 153, 155,
157, 158, 165
Dungeons & Dragons, 54
Dyer, Natalie, 141

Enron, 148
E.T. the Extra Terrestrial
(Spielberg), 14, 37, 46, 47,
54, 87, 110, 112, 113, 115;
Elliot, 111; Mary, 31
Exorcist, The (Friedkin), 104

Facebook, 9
Fanning, Shawn, 9
Fast Times at Ridgemont High
(Heckerling), 84
feminism, third-wave, 139
Ferris Bueller's Day Off (Hughes),
14, 46, 49, 54, 64–65, 76–81,
95, 137, 162, 171; Cameron,
26, 27, 46, 79–80, 142; Ferris
Bueller, 26, 77–81, 92–93,
134; Jeanie, 106; Principal
Rooney, 47, 51, 52, 77–80,
92, 106; Sloane, 29, 78, 134

Generation X: birth years, 10;
economy, perception of
and interactions with, 8, 19,
59–96; family, perception
of and interaction with, 8,
12 15, 16, 18, 19, 21, 23–57; as
"forgotten" generation, 3;
government, perception of
and interaction with, 9, 20,
97–123; lexical origins, 3;
as "missing" generation, 3;
stereotypes of, 6–7
Generation X (Coupland), 4–5
Ghostbusters (Reitman), 18, 55;
Venkman, 154; Winston,
153–54
Glover, Crispin, 9, 82
Google, 9
Goonies, The (Donner), 14, 15, 64,
66–67, 95, 104, 109, 136,
137, 162; Brand, 36, 68, 69,
71, 72, 79, 89; Chunk, 106;
Mikey, 36, 48, 89, 90, 91,
150; Mouth, 90–91
Grant, Barry Keith, 13
Great Recession of 2008, 125–26,
128–31
Gremlins (Dante), 14, 47, 77,
87, 88, 95, 104; Billy, 106,
109; Mrs. Deagle, 67–68;
Mr. Hanson, 50, 53; Mrs.
Harris, 67
grunge music, 11

Hampton, Fred, 152
Heathers (Lehmann), 159
Hudson, Ernie, 154

Ice Cube (artist), 11
Idol, Billy, 4

independents (political affiliation), 148
institutional cynicism, 20, 44, 57, 63
Internet Movie Database (IMDb), 14
intersectionality, 126–27, 138–40, 159

King, Rodney, 102–3
King, Stephen, 15

latchkey children, 9–10, 19, 34, 38
Leto, Jared, 10
Linklater, Richard, 6
Louis CK (Donegan), 139

Madoff, Bernie, 148
"Material Girl" (Madonna), 83
Matsu, Kono, 130
McCain, John, 149
Me Too Movement, 125–27, 138, 141, 143, 148, 151, 157, 160
Millennials, 5, 8, 9–10, 18, 23, 30, 63, 124, 129, 131–32, 135, 149, 151
Mondale, Walter, 98
Montauk Project, 114
Musk, Elon, 9
My So-Called Life (Shafrir), 10

Naked Gun (Zucker), 103
Napster, 9
National Lampoon's European Vacation (Heckerling), 83
Nevermind (album), 54
Night of the Comet (Eberhardt), 83

Nightmare on Elm Street (Craven), 14, 28, 47, 87, 104, 105; Freddy, 48, 107–8, 116
Nirvana (band), 11

Obama, Barack, 149
Occupy Wall Street Movement, 125
Omen, The (Donner), 104
One Crazy Summer (Holland), 66
Oregon Trail Generation, 10
Oswalt, Patton, 124

Page, Larry, 9
patriarchy, toxic, 139–41
Pavement (band), 54
Paypal, 9
Pearl Jam (band), 11
Pixies, The (band), 54
Police Academy (Wilson), 103
"Power of Love, The" (Huey Lewis), 82
Pretty in Pink (Deutch), 95; Duckie, 77–78
Public Enemy (band), 11

Rainbow Coalition, 152
Reagan, Ronald: American Dream, vision of, 131; Back to the Future, affinity for, 101, 117; economic policies, 59–60, 63, 64, 69, 90, 99; "Morning in America" (campaign commercial), 98, 100–101, 103;

presidency, 23; "Reagan
    revolution," 9; reelection
    campaign, 97–99; social
    policies, 93; voodoo eco-
    nomics, 64, 66
Reaganomics, 65
Reality Bites (Stiller), 11
Red Oaks (television series), 64
Reiser, Paul, 115
Replacements, The (band), 54
Republicans, 148–49
Rosemary's Baby (Polanski), 104
Ryder, Winona, 159

Saturday Night Live (television
    series), 124
Say Anything (Crowe), 95
"Should I Stay or Should I Go"
    (The Clash), 55
Silents (generational term), 7
slackers, 6–7
Slackers (Nicks), 6
Soundgarden (band), 11
Spacey, Kevin, 139
Spielberg, Steven, 15, 31
Stand by Me (Reiner), 14, 15, 16,
    25, 120, 160–63; Chris, 26,
    52, 136; Gordie, 26, 27, 136,
    161; Teddy, 26, 161
Star Trek (television series), 55
Star Wars (Lucas), 55
Stranger Things (television series)
    Characters: Barb, 18, 74,
    114; Becky, 39–40; Billy,
    29, 30, 31, 47, 53, 155; Bob,
    35–36, 44–45; Byers family,
    32–36; Dr. Owens, 43, 112,

114–16, 119, 121; Dustin,
    17, 31–32, 48, 78, 144, 146,
    147, 156; Eleven, 15, 23, 29,
    32, 37–46, 52, 83, 113–17,
    120, 136, 142–46, 152–53;
    Erica, 143–44, 146, 153,
    156, 158; Jonathan, 28, 30,
    32, 34, 35, 47, 71–73, 114,
    137–38, 140–41, 147, 158,
    163; Joyce, 29, 32–36, 44,
    45, 53, 71, 74, 85, 112, 113,
    115, 117, 136–40, 143–45,
    150, 153, 158; Kali, 41–42,
    116, 152; Karen, 29, 32–34,
    36, 45, 46, 71, 119, 136–40,
    144–45, 158; Lucas, 28,
    153–56, 158; Max, 31, 38,
    42, 46, 47, 83, 142, 145,
    146, 155, 156; Mayor Kline,
    150; Mike, 18, 28–30, 32,
    34, 36, 42, 44, 55, 69, 72,
    83, 136, 146, 147, 153–54;
    Mr. Clarke, 52–53; Mrs.
    Henderson, 32; Nancy,
    28–29, 32, 46, 48, 69–70,
    72–73, 85, 92, 108, 114, 116,
    136–38, 140–41, 143–46,
    158; Papa, 37, 39, 40, 114;
    Robin, 71, 143–45, 147,
    156; Sheriff Hopper, 32–33,
    37–40, 42–46, 85, 92, 109,
    112–13, 115–16, 119, 120, 121,
    145–46, 150, 152–53; Steve,
    16, 47, 70–71, 143, 147, 156;
    Suzie, 17, 29, 71, 85, 143,
    144, 146; Ted, 29, 32, 93,
    99, 119, 144; Terry (Mama),

4, 39–40, 43; Wheeler family, 32, 33, 36, 37, 57, 69, 83, 133; Will, 15, 30, 32, 34–36, 72, 112, 114–16, 117, 119–21, 136, 145–46, 147

Season One Episodes: "Chapter One: The Vanishing of Will Byers," 34, 112; "Chapter Three: Holly Jolly," 34; "Chapter Seven: The Bathtub," 119

Season Two Episodes: "Chapter One: MADMAX," 38, 70, 163; "Chapter Two: Trick or Treat, Freak," 36, 38, 154; "Chapter Four: Will the Wise," 38–40, 114; "Chapter Seven: The Lost Sister," 41, 42, 116, 152

Season Three Episodes: "Chapter One: Suzie, Do You Copy?," 29, 71, 85; "Chapter Two: The Mall Rats," 85, 92; "Chapter Three: The Case of the Missing Lifeguard," 45, 147; "Chapter Four: The Sauna Test," 72, 113, 140, 141; "Chapter Five: The Flayed," 153; "Chapter Six: E Pluribus Unum," 146; "Chapter Seven: The Bite," 33, 89; "Chapter Eight: The Battle of Starcourt," 84, 113, 143

Summer Rental (Reiner), 66

Thirteeners, 3
Tribe Called Quest, A (band), 11
Twitter, 9

U2 (band), 54

Wall Street (Stone), 95
Weinberg, Mark, 101
Weinstein, Harvey, 139
Weird Science (Hughes), 84
White, Micah, 131
Willie Wonka and the Chocolate Factory (Stuart), 132
World War II, 4, 25, 60, 114
WorldCom, 148

Xennials, 10, 15

Zemeckis, Robert, 117
Zero Population Movement, 104
Zuckerberg, Mark, 9

About the Author

Photo credit: Nate Callens

Melissa Vosen Callens is a self-proclaimed Xennial and watches *Fast Times at Ridgemont High* every time her TIVO records it, despite owning two copies. Vosen Callens is currently an associate professor of practice in communication at North Dakota State University, Fargo. Her writing can be found in *Dialogue: The Interdisciplinary Journal of Popular Culture and Pedagogy*, *English Journal*, *Communication Teacher*, and *A Sense of "Community": Essays on the Television Series and Its Fandom*, among other publications.

www.ingramcontent.com/pod-product-compliance
Lightning Source LLC
Chambersburg PA
CBHW031135270326
41929CB00011B/1632